.H93
1989

CHRISTIANS
— IN A —
SEX·CRAZED
CULTURE

CHRISTIANS
— IN A —
SEX·CRAZED
CULTURE

BILL HYBELS

VICTOR BOOKS ®
A DIVISION OF SCRIPTURE PRESS PUBLICATIONS INC.
USA CANADA ENGLAND

Recommended Dewey Decimal Classification: 248.4
Suggested Subject Heading: CONDUCT OF CHRISTIAN LIFE

Library of Congress Catalog Card Number: 88-62851
ISBN: 0-89693-495-0

CONTENTS

To Rich and Betty Schmidt—

capable co-laborers, whose marriage has been a model for mine.

Acknowledgments

I offer the elders, staff, and board members of Willow Creek Community Church my deepest appreciation for challenging me to research and teach the difficult and delicate subject matter in this book. I'm thankful to my wife, Lynne, for her permission to share openly some of the secrets of our lives. I'm especially grateful to Rob Wilkins and Pat Baranowski for their 11th hour assistance with manuscript revisions.

INTRODUCTION

Why another book on sexuality? Don't we know just about everything there is to know about sex? Hasn't everything that could possibly be known been written and documented already? Perhaps that's true, but no one can claim that our familiarity has diminished our interest. Our sexuality remains an ever-fascinating aspect of who we are.

It is a subject we can't seem to get enough of! Our bookstores are filled with manuals, magazines, and books concerning sexual topics. Movie studios and producers bank on the fact that people will come to see their latest movie project because it contains some degree of sexual excitement. Television and radio programs are liberally filled with visual and word pictures designed to grab our attention. Song lyrics are woven with sexual themes to capture our fancy. Advertising purposefully markets wares by associating products and services with sex. Unquestionably, we are living in a sex-crazed society.

Notably, the marketplace doesn't use its sexually-based strategies without justification. Like it or not, sex sells.

Why is that true? What is it about sexuality that is so powerful? Perhaps it is because relationships, particularly those with the opposite sex, are *very* important to us. Not surprisingly, magazine surveys, psychology books, and one-on-one conversations with people reveal that relationships rank at the top of our "most-important-things-in-life" lists. We are relational creatures.

And we are sexual creatures. This is no accident. The mysterious physical attraction between the sexes was originally and perfectly designed by God. Like everything God created, it was, and is, good. Yet ever since the Creation, God and all His dominion has faced an adversary. Not content to abide in the will of God, Satan has determined to oppose God's goodness and to destroy the precious creatures whom God treasures and loves— us. In his quest for destruction, the evil one has found powerful ground on which to unloose his schemes: the human mind.

We have often heard that the most important sexual organ in the body is the mind. The healthy management of our sexual desires is dependant upon how we process matters in this arena. As we are bombarded with sexual stimuli in our worlds and are subjected to a host of opinions on the topic, a mental toll is taken. To avoid danger, we must submit our thoughts to the higher authority of our designer and creator, Jesus Christ. Although a crude analogy, when we neglect God's wisdom concerning the management of our lives, it's akin to a technical operator ignoring the instruction manual on a nuclear reactor. Terribly harmful consequences can result.

How does the world contribute to our views in this area? A discerning look around reveals an increasing preoccupation with sexual matters which do not fall squarely into God's blueprint for healthy relations. Television, radio, magazines, movies, and advertising all exploit the topic (and people), for the purpose of monetary gain.

And the messages they are sending out are not wholesome, to say the least! In addition, an alarming preponderance of pornographic materials is easily available to anyone who wishes to access them. Research demonstrates that such influences are extremely harmful on a number of levels, serving to further distort our images about sex.

It is an easy task for Satan to derail us in the area of sexual temptation. We can see that part of living in this day and age means we will face all sorts of temptation. Especially sexual temptation. And the lure of temptation will often lead to sin. Sin which will harm people, destroy relationships, and taint God's perfect design.

For those of us who are Christians, our deepest desire, our highest calling, indeed, our ultimate goal is to glorify God. We desire to please Him in all we think, do, and say. Therefore, we look to avoid sin at every turn. So what do we do when we are bombarded with the sexual temptations in our world? What do we do with those sexual feelings and thoughts which demand our attention? Are they so powerful that they're beyond our control? When does a sexual thought become a sin and how serious is it? How should single people handle their sexuality? What do you do if you've failed and fallen short of God's expectations?

These are important questions which deserve to be answered. Even with the wealth of sexual information available to us, and with all our liberated thinking, we have much to learn. We still have doubts, fears, and troubles concerning our sexual worlds; some of us have bruises and scars related to sexuality gone awry. And we are often quite confused about the differing kinds of information available. So, where do we look for the answers to these questions, and when we think we've found them, how do we know if they're truly God's answers? Thankfully, God hasn't left us ignorant or defenseless.

This book is not intended as an exhaustive study on the subject of human sexuality, but rather an attempt to raise our consciousness about the fact that, despite the sexual excesses and craziness in the world today, God knew what He was doing on that creation day when He made man and woman! God has great purpose and interest in the sexual dimension of our humanity. And the Bible remains the definitive word on human nature and human living, even in something as intimate as our sexuality. With such wisdom, we can negotiate a life which is pleasing to Him, resulting in great fulfillment and satisfaction for us.

It is my hope that we can take a thoughtful look together at what God has to say about this mysterious and exciting thing called sexuality, and at our journey's end, thank Him once again for this remarkable gift.

ONE

A Street Called Desire

The sexual awakening did not begin in the sixties. It began with Adam.

I wish I could go down to the corner video store and
rent a documentary of Creation. I would fast-forward the
video to the sixth day so I could watch God create Adam
out of the dust of the ground. Then I would fast-forward
it to the point where God said it was no longer good for
Adam to be alone in the Garden. We read in Genesis 1
that God saw Adam in his aloneness and said, "This isn't
a good thing. Adam is enjoying the Garden and the animals are all around, but he is lonely." I would watch
with great interest while God put Adam into a deep sleep
and fashioned a woman. Then I would zoom in on Adam's face to see his expression when he awoke. When
Adam blinked his lids, sat up, shook his head to get his
senses back, and then spotted this new creature called
woman, that was the first sexual awakening.

When we read the first chapters of Genesis we learn
that human sexuality is neither an accident nor an over-
sight. It's part of God's design. When He created man
and woman, He created them to be attractive to one an-

other. It is not evil for men and women to find each other appealing.

I spent the first eighteen years of my life in a church that never devoted even one Sunday to explaining that human sexuality is a gift from God and that God meant it to be good. Instead, I heard a steady tirade of warnings about the misuse and abuse of sexuality. I heard that I could twist it, make it a negative thing, and that it could destroy me. Therefore, whenever I sensed some kind of resonance with a person of the opposite sex, I immediately thought something must be very wrong with my feelings. I was sure that if I thought too long about my desires, something awful would happen to me. Today I believe I was dealt a great disservice by that church.

To avoid this confusion with my own two children, I have taken great pains to make them comfortable with their own sexuality. To Shauna, my twelve-year-old daughter, I have said, "Honey, if you see a boy at school and you have a curious fascination with him, that's a good thing. God built you to be like that. And He gave you those feelings for a purpose." To Todd, my nine-year-old son, I have said, "If there's a little girl with pigtails that runs around your school and you feel there's something special about her, that's fine. The older you get, the more you'll understand what those feelings are all about."

Though God intended our sexuality to be freely enjoyed as His gift, there are evil elements which threaten His perfect design. For example, all of us drive down the street called Desire. We can't avoid it because it's on the way to church, school, work, and every other place we go. Besides, it's a pleasant drive, one we all enjoy. Along the street called Desire we encounter people whom we are particularly attracted to. There is nothing wrong with this appeal. Physical attraction to the opposite sex is not sin.

Human sexuality is not evil. It is God's gift. Out of our sexuality come feelings that lead us into deep and caring relationships. Expressed within biblical parameters, sexuality brings mutual fulfillment and intimacy that gives great pleasure, which I believe is the fundamental reason for expressing sexuality in marriage. Pleasure first, procreation second.

As long as we stay on the street called Desire, we can enjoy a safe and fascinating ride. But we must drive carefully because it branches off into dangerous territory. These branches can be deceiving; they look much like the main road, but they lead farther and farther from purity.

The first is called Temptation Drive. We all come to it eventually. Even after we are happily married it is not uncommon to meet someone for whom we feel a heightened sexual affinity. These people make our hearts beat a little faster, and we're always conscious of their presence. They represent a kind of vulnerability, a threat, and that can be trouble if we don't handle it right. But we still haven't sinned. Being around people for whom we feel a heightened level of sexual affinity is not wrong.

But if we turn into Temptation Drive, we've started down a road that leads to trouble. Temptation Drive looks much like the beautiful street called Desire, so we can go quite far before we realize we are on the wrong road. Most of us don't figure it out until we come to the intersection of Temptation Drive and Decision Avenue. We know we can take Decision Avenue back to the safety of the main road, but by this time we're enjoying the ride so much that we don't want to go back. We're to the point where we want to act out some of our sexually charged feelings.

We must determine where our ultimate values lie. The value system of the world and that of the Word of God collide violently at this intersection. The wisdom of the world says that sexual appetites are to be indulged.

They're like physical appetites: when we're hungry, we eat; when we're thirsty, we drink; so when we feel sexual desire, we can indulge. I have even heard sexual experts say that repressing sexual desires is a negative psychological experience that can damage our psyches and leave us confused and unhappy for long periods of time. To avoid this unpleasantness, they advise us to break the biblical boundaries.

But God's Word says something different. It says that only when we stay within those boundaries, the boundaries of marriage, can we express love, tenderness, and caring in a meaningful way. Outside of those boundaries, the expression of human sexuality can devastate all involved.

When our highly charged sexual feelings are pounding for release, the Bible does not counsel us to deny their existence. It never says that self-deceit is a good thing. Rather, we should manage them and seek to understand what is causing them. The Bible says we should be as wise as serpents and gentle as doves. We can begin by asking ourselves why we are sexually attracted to others. Is it because we have some unmet needs in our lives? Or is there something in our marriage that we're not dealing with? Might it be that it's easier to fantasize about someone else than to work out problems with our spouse? Or perhaps some have a good relationship with their spouse, but childishly want more. Even more than God intended for them to have. Some people are just sexually greedy. Those who are single might have needs for love or self-esteem that accentuate sexual feelings toward someone they think can meet those needs.

Although the Bible doesn't say to deny heightened sexual feelings, it doesn't say to run out and express them either. In your mind, examine them instead. Seek to understand them. Many have found it helpful to talk to a close friend who will hold them accountable. When we feel especially vulnerable, it helps to confide in someone to whom we can say, "I'm wrestling with temptation in my life. Please help me understand what's going on and hold me accountable so I don't act on it."

Nearly all of us, at one time or another, will meet people other than our spouses to whom we feel a powerful sexual attraction. Some of us, in an attempt to protect ourselves from further temptation, will change jobs, churches, or refuse to go where that person will be. But in the long run, that is not the best solution because wherever we go to escape one person, we will meet others to whom we're attracted.

This means we must make peace with our sexuality. We must acknowledge our sexual feelings and learn to live in harmony with them. At Decision Avenue we go through the painful process of value clarification. It is there that we learn what our true values are.

Some people will work through their feelings, begin to understand them, and learn to keep a safe distance from the people that represent the most danger. Others will learn to stay detached from their feelings so they don't have to deal with perpetual confusion or obsessive temptations. Other people will negotiate their feelings biblically and lead happy, fulfilled lives. And other people will choose to go further down Temptation Drive.

It eventually leads to a wilderness full of deep weeds and dangerous beasts. Following this road leads to big trouble. Randy Alcorn, a pastor of a small group ministry in an Oregon church, wrote (and I paraphrase): "Whenever I feel particularly vulnerable to sexual temptations, I find it helpful to write out what effects, what consequences, my actions could have. Here's what I write: If I go farther down this road, I will probably grieve the One who redeemed me. I will probably drag His sacred name into the mud, which has happened in recent days with a religious leader. One day I will have to look Jesus, the righteous Saviour, in the face and give an account of my actions. If I go farther I will probably inflict untold hurt on my wife, who is my best friend and who has been faithful to me. I will lose my wife's respect and trust; I will hurt my beloved daughters. I will destroy my example and credibility with my children. I might lose my wife and my children forever. I could cause shame to my family. I could lose self-respect. I could create a form of guilt awfully hard to shake. Even though God would forgive me, would I ever be able to forgive myself? I could form memories and flashbacks that could plague future intimacy with my spouse. I could heap judgment and endless difficulty on the person with whom I committed adultery. I could possibly reap the consequences of diseases like gonorrhea, syphilis, herpes, or AIDS. Maybe I could cause a pregnancy, and that would be a lifelong reminder of my sin. Maybe I would invoke shame and lifelong embarrassment on myself."

Smart man. Maybe we all need to write a list like that and put it on the door of our heart so we don't go any farther. Because from here on it gets increasingly difficult to turn back.

The extravagant risk-takers in our midst will say, "This road doesn't scare me. I'm going to keep driving to see where it leads." And so they continue to the next area. It's called Fantasyland. This is where our minds shift into high gear. We manufacture vivid sexual scenarios, and then we create exciting dreams and fantasies to play out on the stage our minds have made. We think we're safe because nobody knows what's going on. And even the experts say there's no harm in it. It's simply mental preoccupation.

But spending a lot of time fantasizing allows several dangerous things to happen. First, we lose valuable thought time that would be better spent on figuring out ways to love God with all our heart, soul, mind, and strength and on advancing His kingdom. Second, people dedicated to their marriages waste time fabricating scenarios that better not ever happen, instead of finding ways to improve their relationships with their spouses. And third, the more time they spend in Fantasyland, the harder it is to enter into legitimate relationships because reality can never live up to fantasy.

Eventually, most people who spend a lot of time in Fantasyland will find themselves in Flirtation Café. We begin changing our schedules to make sure we're around the person we're fantasizing about. We start saying confidential things to each other that we have no business saying. Then we ask questions with double meanings to see if we can measure the other person's sexual interest in us. And flirtation leads to touching. A lingering handshake. A friendly embrace that becomes more than friendly.

Once we become comfortable in Fantasyland, it is even more unlikely that we will have the sense or the strength to turn back to the world of reality. Fantasy becomes reality to us, and so we are easily deceived. We begin to believe what we see at the movies and what our desires tell us—that we can find happiness only in satisfying our sexual appetites. Our wild imaginations tell us what will make us happy, and we reason that it must be good.

Before we know it we are in Passion Park. This is where fantasy returns to reality. For a while it's a pleasant reality. We enjoy it as much as television and movies tell us we will. But this reality has a bitter aftertaste. Hollywood lies. Almost every person I have ever known who ended up in Passion Park has been wounded beyond words and has wounded other people beyond words. Almost without exception, those I have met who have ended up there have said they would do anything to be able to retrace their steps.

It is not a new remorse. David, after his affair with

Bathsheba, wrote: "My iniquities are gone over my head; As a heavy burden they weigh too much for me. My wounds grow foul and fester. Because of my folly, I am bent over and greatly bowed down; I go mourning all day long. For my loins are filled with burning; And there is no soundness in my flesh. I am benumbed and badly crushed; I groan because of the agitation of my heart. . . . My strength fails me; And the light of my eyes, even that has gone from me. My loved ones and my friends stand aloof from my plague; And my kinsmen stand afar off. . . . I am ready to fall, And my sorrow is continually before me. For I confess my iniquity; I am full of anxiety because of my sin" (Ps. 38:4-8, 10-11, 17-18).

About two years after I became pastor of Willow Creek Community Church, a couple from the church called me to their house about midnight one night. They had both gotten involved in adulterous relationships, and they wanted me to sit down in their family room and explain to their two children, a six-year-old and a four-year-old, that their family was going to break up because Mom and Dad had found better partners. Intending to be both calm and professional, I picked up the children and started explaining what was going to happen. I continued talking while the surprise on their faces turned to tears, and then I too started crying. I wanted to look at those parents and say, "Look what's going on. Is your pleasure worth this? What good is sexual pleasure that scars these precious kids for the rest of their lives? Is it that good?"

Many people say that adultery and fornication are where sin starts. But they're not. They are where sin culminates. The sin started at Decision Avenue. The minute we choose to continue to Fantasyland, sin starts. Fantasizing, flirting, touching, and rendezvousing are sin. Adultery and fornication are the culmination.

Some people indulge their sexual appetites so often and with such regularity that not even the bed of the adulterer satisfies them eventually. They move beyond Passion Park to Perversion Alley. These people have allowed their desires to lead them by the nose, and now they have no control over their lust. They get involved in such perversions as pornography and child abuse to satisfy their out-of-control sexual desires.

God designed our wonderful, curious, fascination with people of the opposite sex that leads to exciting relationships and intimate fulfillment in marriage. But when we profane what God meant to be holy, we shatter ourselves and each other with the very gifts God meant to be beautiful.

T W O
Human Sexuality: Design or Default?

On a sweltering August evening in the late '60s , eight
other teenage boys and I tried to ignore the heat long
enough to drift off to sleep after a day's work at a Christian camp. The other seven dealt only with the tempera-
ture, but insecurity intensified my insomnia. They were
veteran workers. I was the rookie. They were all older
and wiser; I was the neophyte. They did the glamorous
work; I scrubbed pots and pans.

The more I thought about being the odd man out, the
more I scrambled to come up with a way to prove myself
to the other guys. I couldn't imagine living this way all
summer in this cramped cabin. So I began to think about
what I could do to gain their respect, to become one of
the guys. Then an idea hit me and I broke the silence.
"How would you guys like to see a movie?" I asked.

"A what?"

"I said a movie."

"Yeah, sure," they said, almost in unison. "I'm sure
we're going to see a movie. Dream on, rookie."

I looked at one of the boys who was my friend, and he
understood my silent message. Without saying another

word we got out of bed, put on some shorts, ran from the cabin, and started our late-night movie caper. We had to hide from the camp staff because we weren't allowed to leave our cabin after taps. Staff members would lurk in the shadows and watch for any movement. Then they would shine their spotlights on the lawbreakers and sentence them to a week or two of quarantine.

We made it to the mess hall and got in by working the lock open with a credit card. Using only the dim light of my flashlight, we located a projector and a screen. Finally we even found the films—a selection of twenty or thirty reels. I shone my flashlight along the racks and squinted at the titles. "The Indianapolis 500 Highlights of 1963." "The World Series Highlights of 1965." The Moody science film "Icebergs in the North Atlantic." Suddenly a title way in the back of the rack caught my eye. My heart started pounding. I started to sweat profusely. My throat went dry. My flashlight vibrated. The title was "Emergency Childbirth."

My partner in crime, who later became a full-time staff member with me at Willow Creek Community Church, and I collected our treasures and tiptoed through the shadows all the way back to the cabin. We set up the equipment without revealing the title of the film.

"It's showtime!" I finally announced, sensing that their respect for the rookie was growing.

"Showtime!" they squealed. "You're kidding. Where'd you get that? You broke into the mess hall? You didn't get caught on the way back? You're all right, rookie."

You ain't seen nothin' yet, I thought. I flipped on the projector. The test-pattern counted down—three, two, one. And there on the screen appeared the two magic words: "Emergency Childbirth." The guys went wild. I could have been elected to public office. I was the hit of the party. And then everyone grew deathly silent as the first picture showed the silhouette of a female figure. Five minutes into the film I knew I had become one of the guys.

Toward the end it showed an uncut, unedited view of a real woman giving birth. Half of the guys had their heads under their pillows; the other half were pleading with me to turn it off. But what a memory that was! That episode embedded itself in my mind. I can bring it all back as though it happened yesterday.

I suspect that nearly everyone reading this book can recall his or her first significant sexual memories as vividly as I can recall some of mine. The whole subject of human sexuality is one of the most sensitive areas in the human personality.

A Sensitive Matter

Our sexuality is inextricably bound into and woven through our self-concept. We cannot think of ourselves apart from who we are sexually. Some people project themselves as being sensual or sexy in order to gain attention. Others feel unattractive or unsexy and, therefore, consider themselves insignificant. Some people keep feelings about their sexuality locked up. Some feel threatened by them. Others are embarrassed.

A Matter of Curiosity

Sexuality is also a topic of almost endless curiosity. There seems to be a perpetual mystique about the subject. Kids learn early in life that there is a mystique about sexuality. When a three-year-old boy asks, "What's this, Mom?" Mom says, "That's your eye." "What's this, Mom?" "That's your nose." "What's this, Mom?" "That's your mouth." "What's this, Mom?" That's your chin." "What's this, Mom?" "That's your chest." "What's this, Mom?" "That's your belly button." But when he points between his legs and asks, "What's this, Mom?" Mom passes out. She knew he was heading south. She knew what was coming, but she was unprepared. She didn't know what to say.

One lecturer on human sexuality asked his audience to list names that parents assigned to their children's sexual organs. The list was hilarious. Kids are bright. They learn early that noses are one thing, eyes are another, and that a certain part of the human anatomy falls into a whole different category.

I have to blush a bit myself. I was in the bathroom with the door not quite shut when our daughter, then two or three years old, cruised by. She stopped, backed up, and asked, "What's that, Dad?" Being the mature, well-adjusted, open-minded father that I am, I said to my wife, "Lynne, your daughter has a question that you girls need to talk about."

Our son gave me my first chance to teach sex education when he was three. Our family had stopped at a small, very quiet restaurant for breakfast. Two business-men sitting at the next table were the only other people in our area of the dining room. The waitress brought our menus, asked if we wanted coffee, stayed just a few seconds, and left. As she was leaving, Todd said, without embarrassment, "Gee, Dad, she has big _____" and used a colloquialism for breasts that I didn't even know he knew. The two businessmen almost fell off their chairs. Lynne's eyes told me it was my turn to handle the sex-ed matter.

I knew this was an important moment in my son's life, so I thought for a moment about how I should react. Finally, trying to be cool, I said, "Son, your dad noticed that too. It's okay to notice that type of thing, but girls get embarrassed if you talk about it. You have to talk about that sort of thing to just us men when we're alone."

Some may question my wisdom on this point, but I believe that from the beginning we need to be as honest and straightforward with our children as possible. They learn very quickly that there is a mystique about this area, and we need to keep a balance between making it unduly mysterious and overloading them with unnecessary facts.

Junior high and high school students are in a perpetual state of curiosity about sexuality. Almost every conversation has sexual connotations. They search for books or magazines that will give them information about something they know very little about. Boys establish black markets for used *Playboy* magazines, and parents often call and tell me with horror that they found a *Penthouse* or a *Playboy* magazine hidden in a bedroom closet. They have no idea what to do.

Teenagers aren't the only curiosity hounds. Even adults who have healthy sexual relationships with their spouses fall prey to the sexual mystique. Titles that sell magazines invariably speak to our innate sexual curiosity: "How to be a better lover," "Overcoming romantic jealousy," "How to seduce your mate." Even *Reader's Digest* rarely goes a month without an article on human sexuality. Sometimes I wonder how many different ways we can find to discuss the subject.

Sexual Chaos

It is clear: sex pervades our culture. And what God has meant to provide great beauty and fulfillment, the world has trashed. On billboards, televisions, bathroom walls, and Top 40 music, the message is the same: enjoy, indulge. Every day we are bombarded from all sides with sexual missiles. We live in a sex-crazed culture, and we will not change it by sticking our heads in the sand.

During one twelve-week period in 1987, prime-time television programs depicted over 2,000 sexual scenes. Also in 1987, 88 percent of all prime-time television references to sexual intercourse were outside marriage (*Ameri-*

can Family Journal, 1988).

It is a sex-crazed culture, and many people are going crazy. Though it is called "sexual freedom," things have taken a nasty turn. An enormous number of people are living in the bondage of guilt. Sexual sin may bring temporary pleasure, but it also promises long-term grief of a perhaps unequalled intensity. Many people in today's sex-crazed culture are feeling the sting of that guilt.

Not long ago a businessman came into my office and broke down and wept on my desk. Thirteen years ago on a business trip he committed adultery with a woman he met in a lounge. For all those years he carried the burden and the guilt and the horror of it. He told me what it had done to his marriage and that he could barely pray.

"In the middle of some of your sermons sometimes I feel so awful I just want to say, 'God, kill me. Send me to hell. I can't live like this.' "

In *The End of Sex*, author George Leonard said, basically, that we've OD'd on sex and that we're entering the postsex era. Gabriel Brown agrees in principle and wrote a book entitled *The New Celibacy: How to Take a Vacation from Sex and Enjoy It*. Is abstinence the answer? Is that where our guilt and disillusionment are leading us?

I hope not. Instead, I think we need to go back to the beginning and understand that human sexuality was not a bad idea, an accident, an afterthought, or an add-on that malfunctioned and now must be abandoned. Rather, human sexuality in all of its wonder and complexity was God's idea. Right from the start. He wove the threads of human sexuality through the fabric of our personalities. Simply reading the first few pages of God's Word gives us at least two of the reasons God designed us to be sexual creatures.

First, God created us to be sexual creatures for our pleasure; second, He made us sexual for procreation. When I speak on this subject and list the reasons for our sexuality in that order, I always sense an uneasiness spreading through the crowd. I can almost hear them say, "You strained your credibility by telling me that a holy God not only allowed sexuality but planned it. And now you're telling me that He created it primarily for human pleasure and only secondarily for procreation."

To some, those thoughts sound downright sacrilegious. But we find them to be true when we reread God's surprising journal of Creation. Of His work on the first, second, third, fourth, and fifth days, God said, it is good. Of His work on the sixth day, the creation of Adam, He said, it is very good. But in Genesis 2:18, we see startling words for the first time. Something is not good. Part of God's creation is incomplete. "It is not good for the man to be alone." In an act of kindness, compassion, and superb creativity, God made Adam a counterpart; He created woman to end man's aloneness. God created her to be distinctive; she is not an exact duplication of man.

God also ordained friendships with people of the same sex to end our aloneness, and those who are single can derive an enormous amount of pleasure from such relationships. But in the area of pleasure, God seems to be underscoring the wonder and the beauty of the counterpart. God created woman physically and emotionally distinctive from man, and this created an immediate fascination between them. We call this sexuality.

Shortly after meeting Eve, Adam said, "This is now bone of my bones, And flesh of my flesh; She shall be called Woman, Because she was taken out of Man. For this cause a man shall leave his father and his mother, and shall cleave to his wife; and they shall become one flesh" (Gen. 2:23-24).

Human sexuality provides the magnetism that pulls two people together and ends their aloneness. "One flesh" refers not only to sexual intercourse but to emotional intercourse as well. Once bonded, two people become inseparable, intimate, and trusting. And all of that, God says, will bring man and woman great pleasure.

"One of the greatest experiences in my life is to know that my husband is strongly attracted to me sexually, physically," a Christian woman told me. "Just living with that knowledge is important to me." Some people know what she means; others know what they're missing. God is interested in our pleasure. He is interested in making life adventurous as opposed to boring and predictable. He is interested in ending our aloneness.

The second reason God created human sexuality was to perpetuate the human race in the context of loving, secure families.

I have no desire to write a textbook on sex education or human anatomy. I simply want to help people discover the wonder of human sexuality, to give them a new perspective on what God's intent for it is, and to help them better understand and appreciate the Designer behind the system. God loves us and couldn't bear to see us live in perpetual aloneness.

THREE
Sexual Fulfillment in Marriage

After a victorious struggle to stay sexually pure through five years of on-and-off dating, Lynne and I expected our honeymoon to be twenty-four-hour passion. Nobody on the planet could have convinced us that our honeymoon would be anything less than we anticipated. Though we'd had problems in our courtship, lack of passion was not one of them. But our honeymoon was a disaster. We could write a book entitled *We Flopped in Florida*.

To start with, we got so sunburned on the second day we said words to one another that we couldn't relate to during our courtship: "Don't touch me." And with the sunburn came nausea, which does wonders for romance, and then blistering and peeling. After that Lynne got a cold sore from her lip to the middle of her neck, which made her feel great about her personal appearance for the last seven days. She accused me of being insensitive because I laughed. That was our sexual debut.

Our early years of marriage didn't offer much opportunity for improvement. I was a full-time youth minister and full-time student finishing my studies at Trinity College. We had two boarders and their dogs living with us in a two-bedroom, cracker-box house. Lynne had two full-term pregnancies, during which she was sick four to five times a day for nine months. She also had two four-month pregnancies that ended in miscarriages, during which she was just as sick for the entire period. Add to this our all-too-typical inability to communicate openly on this very sensitive subject, and the picture becomes quite clear. We weren't any different from anyone else.

After Lynne had put up with me for eight years, I decided to show my appreciation by arranging a special weekend for the two of us.

Unfortunately, our anniversary celebration wasn't any better than our honeymoon. It exemplified all that can go wrong in the physical relationship in marriage.

When I told a friend of mine who manages a local hotel that I wanted to plan a special anniversary celebration, he said, "Don't worry about a thing. I'll take care of you. You show up; I'll have everything prepared."

I selected a restaurant, and we enjoyed a nice dinner together. Then we made the trip over to the hotel, where we learned that my friend had reserved the honeymoon suite for us. It was the size of about four rooms and it had mirrors everywhere. In the center of the mirrors stood a bed on a platform. A huge Jacuzzi and a sauna filled one corner. Socially, it was positively scandalous; morally, it was absolutely decadent; theologically, it was totally depraved. Physically, it was really fantastic. For the next few hours we enjoyed all the accoutrements. We watched a movie, lit the candles, and generally enjoyed the whole evening together. What a fantastic night.

But time was slipping away. It was almost midnight, so I subtly suggested to the bride and love of my youth that she join me in the bed of marital bliss. Actually, I think I said, "Let's hit the sack, Honey." We blew out the candles, climbed up onto the bed, and looked up at the mirrors. Just as I took her into my arms, she said, "The curtains aren't closed tightly enough."

"But we're on the twenty-fifth floor."

"But I want to be able to sleep in, and light rays will wake me up."

"Please, Honey, can't it wait? I'll fix the drapes later."

My pleading didn't work. Lynne crawled out of my embrace and headed toward the curtains.

"Shall I turn the light on?" I asked.

"No, I don't need the light."

A few seconds later I heard a strange noise followed by a soft "Oh-oh. You'd better turn on the light."

When I did, all I could see was blood pouring down my beautiful wife's face. She had walked into one of the four-cornered mirrors around the bedpost, and the encounter left a deep gash in her forehead.

She said it didn't hurt that bad, but we spent the better part of the night in the emergency room of Northwest Community Hospital where doctors had to use seven stitches to repair the damage.

For many people, their sexual relationship, like our honeymoon and anniversary celebration, hasn't gone according to plan. Perhaps it did at first, but it's not anymore. And few know what to do about it or know where to turn for help. There aren't many choices. And there are even fewer good ones.

The Chicago *Sun Times* has carried an advertisement for a new phone service that offers sexual advice when you call the Playboy Company. But don't bother calling. Informed sources tell me that all you get is a recording. Armchair experts might recommend sex manuals, but they resemble *Popular Mechanics* magazines and are just about as scintillating. Friends want to help, but often they have deeper problems than our own. The church should be able to help, but it's been curiously silent on the subject. And so Christians are as confused as anyone in this area, and many feel very alone.

"It's the only thing we fight about," a friend said to me. "Who would have thought that we, of all people, would have this problem? We were so passionate before our wedding that we could hardly stand being in each other's presence, fearing what it would lead to. Now even an attempt to discuss the issue causes immediate polarization." He looked straight at me and said, "Bill, it's not going to change. I can tell. It's never going to change. It's getting steadily worse, and I know myself well enough to realize that I can't live like this the rest of my life. I don't know what to do; I don't know where to turn."

Fortunately, God's Word is not silent. It offers all kinds of advice for finding sexual fulfillment. In this chapter I focus on three guidelines it gives.

First, develop a proper attitude toward the physical dimension of your marriage. Second, improve the atmosphere in and around your marriage and your home. Third, develop honest communication patterns, especially in the sexual part of your marriage.

A Proper Attitude

People often say that the most important sexual organ in the body is the mind. I agree, and I think God's Word alludes to that also. Our attitudes toward our own sexuality and the sexuality of our spouses will largely determine our actions. Too many people have twisted, distorted, and unhealthy attitudes toward human sexuality, but a steady diet of biblical perspectives will offset them.

In the last chapter we saw that the Book of Genesis reveals that sexuality was God's idea. That it was His divine design. That it was instituted by God and woven into the very fabric of our personalities. As the psalmist says, we are fearfully and wonderfully made (Ps. 139:14), and we should thank God regularly that this is so. We should worship God for the gift of attractiveness, for the gift of fascination with the opposite sex, for the gift of sexual adventure. We must continually remind ourselves that the primary reason God wove sexuality into the fabric of our personalities was to end our aloneness.

God wanted us to communicate affection, trust, and loyalty, but not just verbally, because sometimes words are inadequate. They turn to ashes in our mouths. God designed us in such a way that two people can become so intimate, so trusting, so affectionate, and so loyal that they can be considered one flesh. Physically, emotionally, and spiritually. God's design is magnificent, and we should view it that way. If we follow his guidelines, the sexual dimension of marriage can be one of the most fulfilling and satisfying experiences afforded to husbands and wives.

In *Creative Counterpart*, Linda Dillow cites a survey of 500 Christians. Forty percent of the women who responded indicated that inhibition was the biggest problem in their sexual relationship with their husbands. Some of the men said the same thing. Somehow people have come to the erroneous conclusion that free self-expression in the marriage bed is ungodly, inappropriate behavior. In contrast, Hebrews 13:4 states that the marriage bed is undefiled. God created sexuality to be enjoyed in marriage without the inhibitions that cripple so many couples.

Some of this attitude comes from the church. Immorality has long been considered by the church to be one of the most destructive sins in society, so most of what we hear about it in a Christian setting condemns sexual excess and promiscuity but never teaches a healthy alternative. We never hear about the positive aspects of human sexuality.

The Bible freely speaks of how good sex can be. Solomon poetically expresses the beauty of sexuality in its proper context. In His Word, God is saying in essence, "I designed you to feel sexual feelings. And in the sanctity of marriage I designed you to express them—with gusto and without shame." In fact, in 1 Corinthians 7:3-5, a passage that Christians overlook all too often, the Apostle Paul comes right out and says, "Stop depriving one another." In verse 3, he says that the husband should "fulfill his duty to his wife, and likewise also the wife to her husband. The wife does not have authority over her own body, but the husband does; and likewise also the husband does not have authority over his own body, but the wife does."

In the sanctity of marriage we should serve each other sexually, and we should do it selflessly and shamelessly. In this passage and others like it, it's clear that God's will for the husband and wife is a vital, regular, mutually satisfying physical relationship. It's His plan. It's part of what it means to be an obedient Christian. It's part of what discipleship is all about.

One thing that bothers me a great deal is pick-and-choose Christianity. Some believers treat Scripture as if it were flower petals and they were playing a game of loves-me, loves-me-not. Plucking off one principle after another they say, "I'll obey this; I won't obey this; I'll obey this; I won't obey this."

But God hasn't left those choices up to us. When He reveals His will—whether it's in the area of finances, relationships, or sexuality—we are to obey.

The evil one works to destroy God's design. He knows that a vibrant, mutually satisfying, and creative sex life will bind two people together with cords that cannot break. That bond will produce a healthy marriage and family for another generation. God will be glorified and the evil one will suffer defeat. Many naive Christians play into Satan's hands with their improper attitudes toward sexuality.

In Romans 12:2 Paul says that we should not be conformed to the image of people who have worldly values. Instead, we should allow Christ to totally renew our minds. Some of our minds need to be renewed, especially in regard to God's plan for sex in marriage. Since our minds are the most important sexual organ, once they are renewed we will understand God's attitude toward sexuality. Then His attitude will become our attitude and proper actions will flow from that point on.

But how can we renew our minds in this area?

First, we can meditate on passages of Scripture that speak to this subject, especially 1 Corinthians 7 and Song of Solomon. Look in a concordance to find other passages. Study all the ones that speak to the physical relationship in marriage. Write them down. Study them. Meditate on them.

Second, we can read books written by Christian authors that explain God's plan of human sexuality. Two that I recommend are *Intended for Pleasure* by Ed and Gaye Wheat and *The Gift of Sex* by Clifford and Joyce Penner.

Third, we can ask ourselves some difficult questions. What is my attitude toward sexuality? Is it healthy? Is it correct? Does it need renewing? Will I do anything about it? Do I see it as part of my commitment to Christ? Do I want to be held accountable for how I am serving my spouse sexually? Do I realize what could happen if I don't take this seriously?

Fourth, we can discuss the subject with mature believers. We all need each other, and we must conquer the mentality that says we can talk about anything as long as it has nothing to do with sex. Talking with others helps us identify our problems and strengths and gain a sense of objectivity. It also provides a sense of encouragement and accountability.

Once we're convinced that we need a renewed attitude toward sexuality many of us will think we're ready to race into the bedroom. But that's not the next step. Once

our attitude is in order we must focus on the second
scriptural guideline.

An Improved Atmosphere

Once our attitude is renewed, we need to improve the
general atmosphere in our relationship at home. Men are
notorious for their ability to compartmentalize sexuality.
Men tend to view the physical dimension of marriage as
what takes place between Johnny Carson's monologue
and the late movie. They rarely connect sexuality with
what is going on in the relationship as a whole. Men are
infamous for underestimating and being oblivious to the
overall atmosphere of the relationship. Women, on the
other hand, are very conscious of the context of the sexual relationship. They seem to have a greater need to
sense that all is well beyond the bedroom before they are
interested in what could happen in the bedroom. In other
words, before things in the bedroom will improve, things
outside the bedroom must improve.

Dr. Kevin Lehman wrote a book entitled *Sex Begins in
the Kitchen*. After I saw the title I started paying more
attention to people's kitchens. But he was speaking figu-
ratively, not literally. The point he makes over and over
again is that sex is an all-day affair. What goes on outside
the bedroom contributes throughout the day to what
goes on in the bedroom at night. There needs to be affection, encouragement, respect, servanthood, and meaningful conversation outside the bedroom.

As I watched a couple working yesterday, I kidded the
man a little about the job he was doing. His wife came to
his defense immediately. "My husband does everything
very well," she said.

I thought of all the husbands who would love to hear
that kind of encouragement from their wives. Men feast
on that.

Often I hear men from my church say of their wives, in

their presence, "Doesn't she look great? Look at that dress. Isn't it perfect on her?" Although the praise embarrasses the woman, it also builds her self-esteem and improves their relationship.

On the other hand, if there is no trust, little affection, and very little encouragement, there's likely to be sexual discouragement and breakdown in the bedroom.

Once again it's time to ask ourselves the difficult questions. Am I affectionate? Am I trusting? Do I encourage my spouse? Do I serve my spouse? How can I improve these areas? How else can I improve the quality of our relationship outside the bedroom?

Those who have a proper attitude toward sexuality and a healthy atmosphere beyond the bedroom probably feel ready to hit the sack. Dim the lights. Put on Henry Mancini. Start the fireworks.

Not yet. There's still one more step.

Honest Communication

In *Thoroughly Married*, Dennis Guernsey makes two direct statements that are difficult for readers to swallow. In effect, he says, "Come on, husbands. Come on, wives. Stop the charade. Cut the pretense. Admit it. First, admit that we don't know as much about each other's bodies as we claim we do. And second, admit that we could never make a living being mind readers."

Where did most of us get our knowledge of human anatomy and sexuality? How many have taken graduate level courses on sexuality? Undergraduate? High school health class? Probably not many. Most of us learned from a cousin Eddie who was two years older and had a big mouth. He said he knew it all, but he didn't. I learned from truck drivers and dockworkers. They talked a lot, but didn't know much. Most of us, Guernsey says, need more education. We need to read more to understand even the basic sexuality of our spouses.

But better than reading, he says, is to have frank conversations with our spouses because most of us are lousy
mind readers.

I've been with married couples in restaurants, and the
wife knows exactly what her husband will order, how he
wants it cooked, what kind of salad dressing he prefers,
and what he takes in his coffee. We know a lot about
each other's tastes in food, clothing, entertainment, travel, and politics, but not much about sexual preferences.

We feel free to discuss our likes and dislikes in non-
threatening areas. But when we turn off the lights and
take off our clothes, we become vulnerable. An eerie silence fills the room and we bumble and fumble as we try
to read each other's minds. Too often both partners drift
off to sleep silently wondering what it would be like to
have a sexually fulfilling experience.

Guernsey says we have two choices: learn to communicate or live in ongoing frustration.

Which will it be?

A while back, I decided that I had to do a better job of
communicating with my wife in this area. I spent three
and a half hours writing a letter to her, suggesting in
detail how I felt about our physical relationship and how
I thought it could be improved. I put it in an envelope
labeled "My Christmas List" and gave it to her. "Please,
honey, spend whatever time it takes, but give me your
Christmas list. I want this area of our lives to improve
consistently throughout the years. Our likes, dislikes,
and attitudes are going to change periodically. We've got
to communicate on this."

Just giving her my letter brought about significant im-
provements in our communication patterns. Ephesians
4:15 says that we are to speak the truth to one another in
love.

In summary, I have three practical suggestions:

First, read some books on the subject. We need to do

more reading in this area. The ones I mentioned earlier are good ones to start with.

Second, within the next week or two, write and deliver to your spouse a list of ways to improve your physical relationship. Just say, "I want to communicate better on this. I'm a lousy mind reader and I know you are too. Let this be the beginning of communication."

Third, do what Lynne and I do almost every week. We go out on a date. If we can't schedule a quiet dinner together, we go out for breakfast or lunch. This allows us to get out of the house and away from the children and to focus our attention on each other rather than on all that needs to be done. Those special times together have greatly enriched our relationship.

Remember, we must communicate or live in frustration. Which will it be?

F O U R
What Causes Affairs?

Martha went to a luncheon with ten other women. During the conversation, one boldly asked the others how many had been faithful to their husbands for the duration of their marriages.

"Only one woman raised her hand," Martha told her husband later. Then she hung her head. "And it wasn't me. But I have been faithful to you," she quickly added.

"Then why didn't you raise your hand?" her husband asked.

"Because I was ashamed."

The preceding example from J. Allan Petersen's book, *The Myth of Greener Grass*, demonstrates an important point. People are ashamed of being faithful. Fidelity is out; affairs are in. If marriage doesn't provide all we expect, dream of, and fantasize about, and if it fails to bring the sensory pleasures and fulfillment we think we deserve, many of us think we should be free to go elsewhere. To find greener grass. To enjoy some healthy adultery.

"Healthy adultery" is a term used by Dr. Albert Ellis, a prominent sexologist. He counsels couples, whose romantic love has faded, to commit adultery to rejuvenate their relationship. Unfortunately, he is not the only expert offering this type of counsel.

We used to talk about guilt, pain, destruction of self-esteem, deceit, and consequences when we spoke of adultery. Now we don't even say adultery. We say they are having an affair or developing a meaningful relationship with someone outside of marriage. We want to make it sound less repugnant, less serious, less sinful.

We are making it everything except less frequent. Adultery is happening in record numbers. Statistics vary, but most experts now say that two thirds of all married men and half of all married women will commit adultery some time during their marriages. Women who enter the work force are more likely to have an affair than those who stay at home. So many predict that it's just a matter of time before both men and women will be at about the same level of unfaithfulness.

Only limited studies have been done concerning adultery among Christians. But initial findings have been shocking. Author Eve Baguedor sums up the situation quite well with the title of her magazine article *Is Anyone Faithful Anymore?* And so does the song title "Doesn't Anybody Stay Together Anymore?"

Just before Lynne and I left for our summer break one year, a friend gave me a copy of *The Myth of the Greener Grass*. I stuffed it in my briefcase and took it with me. After reading the first thirty pages, I said to Lynne, "This is a good book." When I was about halfway through, I said, "Lynne, this is a great book." When I finished it, I said, "Everybody should read this book."

That single book answered many of the questions I had been struggling to answer on the subject of adultery: What causes affairs? Why are they happening in record numbers? Is it a lack of biblical knowledge? Do people not think it's wrong anymore?

I couldn't quite bring myself to believe that it was the latter. I think we all know, though we may not be willing to admit it, that there's something wrong with adultery. We don't have to go far into God's Word or hear many sermons to learn that God has some very negative feelings about adultery. The seventh commandment states it as clearly as anyone can: "You shall not commit adultery" (Ex. 20:14).

It's as simple as that. There are no conditions or escape clauses attached to it. No third party involvement, ever. God never condones it. In fact, in the Old Testament, under Mosaic Law, anyone caught in adultery received the death penalty. And the Pharisees wanted to do the same thing in the New Testament. They dragged a woman into the presence of Jesus and said, "We caught this woman in the act of adultery. We say let's kill her."

Scripture is filled with consistent teaching on this subject. One man, one woman. They are to leave their parents and cleave to each other in a monogamous, permanent marriage. Few people seriously question the biblical position on this subject. Few people commit adultery out of moral ignorance.

Why then, when the consequences are so deadly, do so many people cheat on their spouses?

Petersen says that people cheat for three reasons: (1) emotional immaturity; (2) unresolved conflict in marriage; (3) unmet needs in marriage.

Emotional Immaturity
In the early years of my ministry I did a lot of marriage counseling, and I learned a great deal about what causes the eventual disintegration of a marriage. After only a few sessions, I could usually detect the cause of the tension. And when adultery was involved, I could usually determine why one partner had ended up in another person's bedroom.

In my counseling experiences, I have dealt with three kinds of emotional immaturity.

Forbidden Fruit Syndrome

Before long in my counseling career, I found myself dealing with a couple who had serious problems; the husband had had several extramarital affairs. As I talked with them, I began to probe to find out what was really going on inside their marriage and why the husband had betrayed his wife.

"Tell me," I said, "do you fight with one another? What do you fight about?"

"We don't fight," they agreed.

"OK, do you enjoy being in each other's company?"

"We love being in each other's company. We really do."

"How are things at work?" I asked the husband.

"Things at work are tremendous. I just got a promotion. Things are going very well there."

"How are things at home? I know you have young children. They can cause some conflict. I know about things like that. Are the kids getting you down?"

"No. Not at all," the wife said. "God has given us wonderful kids. That's no source of conflict whatsoever."

I was running out of questions, but I still held my ace. "Well, let's get right down to it," I said. "I hope you're not embarrassed by this question, but how is your sexual relationship?"

"Tremendous," the husband answered. "We have a tremendous physical relationship."

I turned to the wife. "How is your physical relationship?" I asked.

"Super," she said. "Just great. There is no problem in that area at all."

"Maybe one of you has some latent bitterness or anger that's built up over time," I suggested.

"No, we can't identify with any of that," they both agreed.

"What about your in-laws. Do you have a problem with either set?"

"No, we always have a great time at family gatherings."

By this time I was scrambling for ideas. "Does he ever encourage you?" I asked the wife.

"Yes, he's very encouraging."

I couldn't put my finger on a thing. Finally I said, "All right, I want the truth. No more game playing. I'm going to go through the questions once more, and this time I want honesty."

When I asked the questions again, they answered every one the same way, and that time I felt they were telling me the truth. I was stymied until the husband said, almost under his breath, "I guess the whole thing was like forbidden fruit."

A light went on in my mind.

He continued. "She wasn't even attractive. I didn't love her; I didn't want an ongoing relationship with her. It was just like an adventure. And the illegality of it seemed to excite me."

And then all of the lights went on. I used to enjoy watching "Candid Camera" when it was on television. One of my favorite gags was when they would find a busy downtown street near a construction site, drill a three-inch hole through the high wooden fence, and paint a sign over the hole that said, "Do not look through this hole." Then they would put a camera off to the side and wait for people to come by. Those who didn't see the sign would keep walking. But people who saw it would stop, look one way and then the other, and then look right into the hole.

God put Adam and Eve into a garden filled with all kinds of trees. He gave them complete freedom to eat the fruit from all of them except one. So which one did they want? The one they couldn't have, of course, just like all their offspring who followed them. We all want to snack on the forbidden fruit.

I realized that this couple did not have a problem with their relationship; the husband had a problem with emotional immaturity. In many ways he was still an adolescent. He was like a teenager who breaks into his parents' liquor cabinet just because it's locked and he's been told to stay out of it. Or like a high school student who gags on a cigarette because she's been told not to smoke.

This man was simply an overgrown adolescent, and there are a lot of them running around these days. I told his brokenhearted wife what I have been able to tell many other violated spouses: The affair was not your fault. It wasn't that you weren't meeting your spouse's needs. You could not have averted it if you had tried. Emotionally immature people do foolish things, and no one can stop them. Your marriage doesn't have to break up, but your spouse has to grow up or it's going to happen over and over again.

Another kind of emotional immaturity that leads to adultery is low self-esteem. A middle-aged woman who flirts and teases and ends up sleeping with another man may be desperately trying to prove that she's still attractive and desirable.

Even though her husband frequently tells her she is beautiful, she is so immature and has such low self-esteem that she must prove to herself that she is beautiful by testing her appeal with other men.

This also happens with some men who need to relive their high school or college glory days. They have to prove to themselves that they can still attract women. Now that they're not throwing touchdown passes or setting scoring records, attracting women is the only way they know to prove their personal worth. And so they prove it a few times. And they destroy their spouses and their marriages.

Self-Gratification
Another form of emotional immaturity is self-gratification. Adults who were pampered or overindulged as children are more likely to have affairs. As children, they always got what they wanted and never had to stay within any boundaries. When they get married, they expect the trend to continue. But soon the restrictions of a monogamous marriage become too binding and they look for ways to get what they want outside of marriage.

Self-Centered
Those who are wealthy, powerful, or in positions of leadership are also prone to affairs. Pride sets in and they begin to think they can break the rules without consequences.

King David was at the peak of power and political influence when he decided he had the right to take another man's wife. David must have had a "Say yes to the king" campaign going on in Israel. Legally, no one could stop him. As king, he lived above the civil law. But God stopped him. No one lives above His moral law.

Today we see a lot of people, religious leaders included, who think they live above God's moral law. So many people have said yes to them that they can no longer say no to themselves. Government officials, corporate executives, and Christian leaders become enamored with their own power. Since they are the ones making the rules for others, they begin to think they are above the rules they make. But God isn't playing the role of Shrinking Violet. He's made it pretty clear that he's the only one with the power to make and enforce the rules.

For single people, the implications of emotional immaturity are obvious. If you are dating someone who shows symptoms of it, you have an affair-prone person on your hands, so don't jump into marriage. Spend time exploring these areas together until you are sure you are both moving toward emotional maturity.

For those already married to emotionally immature spouses who have been unfaithful, I want to ease the pain by saying, "It wasn't your fault. God knows that. You couldn't have averted it if you had tried. So don't keep rehearsing the past, wondering what you could have done differently. You need to get on with your life. Don't carry that baggage around. It will exhaust you and ruin your life."

Those who sense this immaturity need to stay alert to their vulnerability. If you crave adventure, have a poor self-image, or need affirmation from people other than your spouse, be careful. If you were granted every wish by indulgent parents, have attained wealth, or have achieved power, be vigilant. The evil one wants to destroy the bonds of fidelity in your marriage.

One of the reasons I keep challenging people to give their lives to Christ, to serve God, to be a part of a Bible teaching church, and to get into a discipleship group is not because I want a bigger church. It's because we all need to grow up, and we need each other's help to do it. We need to sharpen each other, challenge each other, and admonish each other. When we become emotionally mature, we take one step toward removing ourselves from the list of affair-prone people.

Unresolved Conflict

If you were to come early to our church on Sunday morning you would hear our band warming up their instruments. The pianist strikes the pitch, and the musicians in turn tune their instruments to that note. If they start before they tune up, it drives them all crazy.

Have you ever been to a recital where a performer sang

about a half pitch flat the whole time? People start fanning themselves and looking for exit doors. The dissonance makes them uncomfortable. Or have you ever driven a car that pulled to one side because it had a front tire out of alignment? The tension exhausts you by the time you get where you're going. Dissonance causes discomfort and anxiety, and people do one of two things to eliminate it. They try to create harmony or they pull away.

When two imperfect people join together in a marriage, dissonance is inevitable. If they don't deal with their dissonance, detachment will follow. Slowly but surely they will pull away from each other. Silence will replace happy chatter, scowls will replace smiles, and walls will replace bridges. Loneliness will set in, then alienation, and one day they will ask, "Who's this stranger I'm living with and why should I perpetuate this charade?" They desperately desire harmony.

When I hear people say, "I found someone at work that I can really talk to," I know they are in trouble. They are running away from the dissonance in their marriage and running toward the harmony of a new relationship. It's only a matter of time before they end up in bed. They're an infidelity statistic waiting to happen.

We either work at conflict resolution or we watch detachment destroy our marriage. I know couples who have been squared off for fifteen years. They haven't come to the center of the ring (except to exchange punches) for a long, long time. They think nothing can resolve their conflict.

Some time ago when Lynne and I were having a conflict in our marriage, I called a friend and asked if we could meet. I bared my soul to this individual. "I just lost perspective," I said. "All I want to do is make a point, and I know God wants me to make peace." After three hours I went home and said, "Lynne, there are some things I'm right about and there are some things I've been wrong about. Thank God for someone else who could give me a little perspective on it." Thanks to the godly advice of a trusted friend, we resolved our conflict.

We need to be the kind of people who do not let unresolved conflict cause detachment, roving eyes, and adultery. We need to work at resolving our differences. If we cannot do it alone, we need to get professional counseling or meet with other believers who know us, love us, and will be honest with us.

We also need to be honest with God. I wish every married person would live by Ephesians 4:26: "Do not let the sun go down on your anger."

Whether our anger lasts an hour, a day, a week, or a year, we need to take off our gloves, get on our knees, and tell God we can't resolve the conflict alone. Only when we are reconciled to Him can we start being reconciled to our spouse.

Unmet Needs

The third reason partners cheat is because of unmet needs. When needs go consistently unmet, the door of infidelity swings wide open. Human beings are a needy group. We see it every time a new baby comes into the world. A baby is totally helpless, totally dependent on its parents to meet its physical, emotional, and psychological needs. I can't count the times my kids have looked up at me and said, "Did I do good, Dad?" "Tell me I did good, Dad." "Am I OK, Dad?" "You still love me, Dad?"

Kids are needy. And adults are just grown-up kids. We have deep inner yearnings. In a way, spouses replace parents as primary need-meeters. Only God, of course, can meet ultimate, eternal, and spiritual needs. And only God can be our ultimate security, peace, and hope. But as spouses we must doggedly determine to meet the ongoing needs of our partners.

We need acceptance. "I Love You Just the Way You

Are" should be the theme song of every married couple. And our conversation should regularly include acceptance statements like the following: "Honey, I know you have idiosyncracies, liabilities, hang-ups, problems, and prejudices, but I'm one person in this world who loves you anyway. I'm hoping that God will continue to transform you into His image, but I'm not going to try to transform you into my image. I love you just the way you are."

We need affirmation. Whenever we exert energy, achieve a goal, or make a major decision, we build our character, and it is important at these times that we receive affirmation from our spouses. "That was a good decision you made." "I admire the character trait that I see developing in your life." "That was quite an achievement; I'm proud of you." "I admire you for standing up for that person." We need to practice rewarding and affirming each other for the good that we do.

Sex should be an expression of our affection for one another. I met a man who says that the demise of his marriage was due to the total disregard of his sexual needs by his spouse. In 1 Corinthians 7:5 Paul says we should stop depriving each other sexually. Sex is more than just a physical act. Other, deeper needs can be met when affection is expressed through sex. Go above and beyond the call of duty.

As much as is humanly possible, marriage partners must strive to be the primary need-meeters in their spouses' lives. We must express needs to one another, discuss those needs, and seek to meet them with all our hearts.

Hope and Help
Adultery is a grievous crime. When we commit adultery we defy the holiness and the character of Almighty God. We commit cosmic treason. We don't think of ourselves

as defiant, but we're saying to God, "I don't care who You are; I'm doing it my way." In Galatians, Paul says, "Do not be deceived, God is not mocked; for whatever a man sows, this he will also reap" (6:7). We can't get away with it. God will not be mocked. Adultery is a crime against God, spouse, and family. So don't do it. Don't even think about it.

But adultery is not the end of the world. Nowhere in Scripture is it called the unpardonable sin. Committing adultery does not condemn people to hell. Forgiveness is available (see chapter 12).

And so is healing. God is capable of rebuilding the shattered life of the faithful spouse. Violated spouse, listen to me. God knows your pain. Nobody else understands the rejection you feel, but He does. And He's compassionate. He wants to be your refuge and your strength. Isaiah 43:4 says you are precious in His sight. He loves you. Though your spouse was unfaithful, God is ever faithful. Turn to Him. Lean on Him. Pour out your heart before Him. He can rebuild shattered lives. Genesis 41:52 states that God can make you fruitful in places of much suffering. Reconstruction is His specialty.

God can totally reconstruct your marriage. Even if it's nothing more than charred rubble, God can rebuild it. He's more dependable than Prudential. You may need Christian counseling. And it will take time. But if you're both willing, day by day, piece by piece, God can lay a new foundation for communication, trust, and sensitivity. He can give you an even deeper love for one another than you ever had before. What the evil one meant for disaster, God can turn into good.

FIVE
How to Affair-Proof Your Marriage

I attended a wedding yesterday and once again heard those famous vows: To have and to hold, from this day forward, for better or for worse, for richer or for poorer, in sickness and in health, to love and to cherish, till death do us part.

Nearly every newly married couple is so committed to one another on their wedding day that the thought of unfaithfulness, adultery, an affair, or any third-party involvement whatsoever is totally preposterous. On wedding days newly married couples can't believe that there could ever be a threat to fidelity.

But just outside the church doors, threats await them. And nearly fifty percent of couples who exchange vows today will be unable to keep them for all their tomorrows.

We need to learn how to take preventative measures. We need to take steps to affair-proof our marriages. I want to challenge you to faithfulness before disaster strikes, before the damage is done, before credibility and trust are shattered, and before God is dishonored.

If you think that an affair could never happen to you,

you are thinking incorrectly. To believe you are immune leaves you wide open and unprotected. First Corinthians 10:12 says, "Therefore let him who thinks he stands take heed lest he fall." Don't be overconfident. Don't live too near the edge.

To affair-proof our marriages we must do three things: (1) affair-proof ourselves; (2) affair-proof our spouses; and (3) affair-proof our lifestyles.

An Affair-Proof Self

If we each affair-proof ourselves, theoretically we reduce the possibility of marital infidelity by fifty percent. That's quite an improvement. And if both partners affair-proof themselves, the chances for infidelity approach zero.

It's easy to talk about marriage because it takes the spotlight off us as individuals and focuses on the mystical union no one can explain. But each partner is responsible for his or her own actions, for his or her own faithfulness. We each need to examine our personal attitudes concerning adultery. Is it on our list of options? Given the right circumstances and the right person, is it a possibility? If it's happened before, could it happen again?

Keep in mind that Scripture says we will one day stand accountable to God, and we will stand in the blazing brilliance of His holiness all alone, not hand-in-hand with our spouses. Scripture never indicates that we will stand in groups or as couples before the throne. According to 1 Corinthians 3:13, 1 Corinthians 4:5, and 2 Corinthians 5:10, each man and each woman will someday stand and give an account of his or her life.

Realizing the responsibility we have, realizing our accountability before a holy God, we need to pledge ourselves to faithfulness. We need to say before God and others that we are making a commitment to absolute fidelity for the rest of our lives, regardless of what our spouses decide.

The evil one leads slowly, subtly, and with uncanny ability to maneuver down the path of infidelity. He has to; he has a tough job. He has to convince people who pledged faithfulness to their spouses that it is better to follow him down the path of unfaithfulness than to stay true to those vows. He has to convince them that there is more excitement in the bedroom of another person than in keeping promises of unending love and commitment.

He doesn't get us there in one easy step. He approaches slowly and quietly. Before we even know he's around, he plants a thought in our minds, the seed of infidelity. As the honeymoon ends, the romance fades, and reality sets in, the seed sprouts. As conflicts arise, professional pressures increase, and communication decreases, the seedling grows. As attractive people come into our lives, the young plant blossoms. The evil one displays it in all its glory. He makes sure we see it everywhere we look, that we smell its lovely fragrance everywhere we go.

We start to wonder what it would be like to have a relationship with persons other than our spouses. We fire our imaginations up, allowing the possibility of our imaginations running away with us.

We cannot insulate ourselves totally. Temptation will come. But what we do with that temptation makes all the difference in the world.

Essentially, we have two choices.

Nurture Temptation
The first choice is easier because it follows the path of least resistance. Nurturing lustful desires requires no moral strength, no moral character. But neither does it build any. Instead of attacking the tempting thoughts, we incubate them. We create all sorts of extramarital scenarios in our minds: romantic evenings, candlelight dinners, sexual encounters. And at that point, temptation becomes sin. When we nurture tempting thoughts, we sin,

and we are one step farther on the road to adultery.

Now that we have so much excitement and romance going on in our mind, our spouse begins to seem dull and unattractive. It is almost impossible to keep these unfair comparisons from negatively affecting our relationship with our spouse. We withdraw. We sense distance and detachment. We become less affectionate because what's going on in our fantasy is more exciting than what's going on in reality.

For all intents and purposes, we're already having an affair. That's what Jesus was talking about when He said, "Everyone who looks on a woman to lust for her has committed adultery with her already in his heart" (Matt. 5:28). When adultery occurs for long periods of time in the mind, it's only a matter of time before it happens in the flesh.

The evil one then lures us with lies. "God won't care," he whispers. "What's one little slip, one little romantic evening? God is forgiving. And no one else will ever find out. It won't affect your marriage. It won't jeopardize your relationship with your children. In fact, it'll be exciting."

Satan is the father of lies. "You are of your father the devil, and you want to do the desires of your father. He . . . does not stand in the truth, because there is no truth in him. Whenever he speaks a lie, he speaks from his own nature; for he is a liar, and the father of lies" (John 8:44).

Steady streams of deception flow from Satan's lips. He's been using deceit and lies to trap people in sin ever since he used them so successfully on Eve in the Garden of Eden. "Eat from the tree," he told her. "God won't care. There won't be any consequences. You won't die. In fact, you'll be like God." Adam and Eve believed his lies, and we've been living with the consequences ever since.

Attack Temptation

The second choice we can make when Satan dons his smock and unpacks his paints is to attack his mental artwork by saying, "I know where these pictures are coming from. Straight from Satan. I know where he's trying to lead me. Straight into trouble. I'm going to call him what he is. A liar. I'm going to dismiss these thoughts. With God's help I'm going to change the direction of my mind. I'm going to control my thought life. I'm going to take my mind down a different road."

I'm ashamed to admit that from time to time I have not always dismissed those thoughts as readily as I should have. I have incubated some ungodly thoughts and I've even listened to Satan's lies. I've heard him say, "God won't care. Lynne will never find out."

By God's grace I've never been unfaithful to Lynne, and I plan to be faithful to her the rest of my life. Why? First, because I love Jesus Christ, who said, "If you love me, keep my commandments."

I consider it the greatest miracle in my life that God would save a person like me, because my heart is so wicked and prone to wandering. I am awed by my salvation and by how God has used me, blessed me, and promised me an eternal home in heaven. I love Christ, and I'm not ashamed to admit it. And He says, "If you love Me, you'll want to keep My commandments." And I love Him, and I want to keep the commandments. Even number seven.

Second, I intend to be faithful because I also love Lynne with all my heart, and I love our kids. The thought of hurting her, of jeopardizing my kids and my family, is abhorrent to me.

And third, I plan to be faithful because I fear the wrath of God. Some people don't fear God. They think they know Him so well that they can predict His response to disobedience. Not me. God surprises me. He has broken out of every box I've ever tried to put Him in.

For instance, I would have been dead wrong if I had been asked to predict God's response to Moses for striking the rock when told to speak to it. Poor Moses had been putting up with a lot of grief from God's people for forty years. I would have expected God to take a more lenient position on Moses' seemingly minor act of disobedience. After all, striking the rock was no new thing. Once before when the people were thirsty, God had told Moses to strike it. I thought God would say, "Moses, I know you're angry, exhausted, and frustrated from all this turmoil. You probably just misunderstood me. Please listen more carefully next time." But He didn't. God was hard-nosed with Moses. He said, "Moses, because you disobeyed me, you'll never see the Promised Land."

I would have been wrong about Nadab and Abihu as well. These two young priests were just starting their ministry. As young men in ministry tend to do, they started playing around a bit. They got a little careless, a little irreverent. And they offered a slightly different kind of incense than God had prescribed in Levitical law. This too seems like a minor offense to me. But it was no laughing matter to God. As they joked around, apparently playing with the incense, God struck them dead.

Uzzah was another biblical character who got a seemingly harsh punishment. He knew that he was not to touch the ark of the covenant, but it was falling off the cart. He reached out his hand to steady it, to keep it from falling to the ground. And God struck him dead.

Even David, whom God loved, got some heavy-handed treatment. Because of his one-night stand with Bathsheba, God took the life of their child.

When I put all of these stories together, I come up with one conclusion. I can't predict what God might do, but I have a sneaking suspicion it could be serious. If I commit adultery, knowing the Word of God as I do and after all that Christ has done for me, God would have a perfect right to chastise me, and I would deserve it. He could take away my wife; He could take the blessing from my ministry; He could smite one of my children; He could take away my health; He could take my life.

Most Christians have a way of finding and memorizing comforting verses that talk about peace, joy, and the abundant life. We should memorize verses like Hebrews 10:31: "It is a terrifying thing to fall into the hands of the living God." This refers to falling into His hand of judgment after disobedience. It is a terrifying thing because we don't know what He might do. We have no concept of how our sin defies His holiness.

Very few people take God's wrath seriously. I'm not saying that we have an angry God or that we ought to live with the sword of Damocles hanging over our heads. But Scripture says we do have a God who can get angry.

But what about people who jump from sack to sack and still everything goes right for them? To that I can only say that God doesn't settle all His accounts in thirty days, or twenty-four months, or five years, or ten decades. God will settle some of His accounts at His throne. To some people He will say, "Depart from Me; go into hell forever and ever; you were a worker of iniquity."

An Affair-Proof Spouse

I don't recommend hiring a private detective to tail suspicious spouses, and I know of no modern-day chastity belts. The only way I know to affair-proof my spouse is to keep my lawn so green that all others look brown. But I see many where the opposite is true. Some lawns are so barren they make a patch of asphalt look healthy.

We should have no fairy-tale illusions about our spouses. The evil one will tempt and seek to deceive every one of them. He is no respecter of persons. When he tries to interest my wife in other men, I want Lynne to say to herself, "This man may be better looking than Bill, and he is certainly richer, but will he be as concerned about my well-being as Bill has been? Will he challenge me and lead me spiritually like Bill has? Will he seek to build my self-image? Will he cheer me on and encourage me to expand my abilities? Will he push me to reach my potential? Will he be as good a father to our kids? Will he be as tender and as affectionate and as pleasing sexually?"

We should try to maintain a sense of freshness about our marriages. Do something out of the routine. Go for a picnic in the winter. Buy roses on an ordinary Tuesday. Check into a Holiday Inn for a weekend. Pick up the game of tennis. Date nights are also a way of keeping vitality in a marriage. They establish a regular time of communication without all the demands of children, job, and other pressures. Leave time for just the two of you.

I want to be the kind of husband who will make Lynne stop and say, "I would be crazy to jeopardize what I have." I want her to say, "Why trade a Corvette for a pair of roller skates? Or a Harley for a Honda?" I want to be so devoted to her that the grass all around us looks brown.

An Affair-Proof Lifestyle

It's no secret that most extramarital affairs happen between close personal friends and coworkers. So it behooves us to choose our friends wisely. Make sure they are as committed to faithfulness in marriage as we are. If we sense they are not, we know to keep a safe distance. And it is never wise to spend much time with people, married or single, who are seeking sexual involvement with us.

Beware of the workplace. According to a leading magazine, "The business atmosphere itself fosters the budding of romance. Everybody's dressed for success, receptionists screen calls, night maids keep things spotless. Expense accounts cover long lunches in four-star restaurants, leisurely drinks after work to talk over the day's events, business trips to luxury hotels complete with room service, hot tubs, and swimming pools. Companies unwittingly promote intimate relationships by setting up work teams that frequently turn out to be male-female. We have a saying around the office that you have to fall in love a bit to work well together."

Cece married right out of high school and didn't work until her late thirties when she took a job to clear up some bills. When she discovered she liked working and had a real knack for computers, she moved from secretary all the way up to designer and brought home three times the salary her husband did. She also became deeply attached to Chuck, another design whiz who had no formal training. She felt she had much more in common with Chuck than with her husband.

"I felt like a fairy tale princess who had to go back to the dungeon every night," she said. "I tried to play the role of good little wife at home to keep the peace, but I often couldn't resist having a drink with Chuck after work. Then I'd get home late and Jack would hit the roof" ("Office Marriages," *Ladies Home Journal*, Oct. '83).

The workplace is fertile ground for extramarital affairs. We need to take preventative measures to keep from developing unhealthy desires. We must take steps to develop accountability.

I have established a set of guidelines to help me avoid situations that could lead to temptation. First, I avoid having lunches alone in restaurants with a woman other than my wife, and I avoid riding alone in a car with another woman. Also, I avoid meeting alone with women in my office without one of my two assistants directly outside my glass-paneled office door. Finally, I avoid traveling without a companion (Lynne, the kids, or a male staff or board member) so that there cannot even be an accusation made pertaining to inappropriate behavior. I'm committed to being alert to any new danger areas, and as I sniff them out, I will add appropriate measures to my list.

If we do not set up guidelines to establish accountability, we are inviting trouble. Recently, a pastor of a major church was exposed in having multiple adulterous relationships. When I asked him how this could have happened, he replied that he had created an environment where he had to answer to no one. And now, after dragging Christ's name through the mud and shattering a once vital ministry, he now realizes that he does have to answer to Someone. He understands, all too late, that God is not mocked.

SIX
Sex and the Single Life

When I was in high school, back in the late '60s, boys had to be part of the car-crazy culture or they were nobodies. Many of my friends worked two or three jobs to be able to buy a car and cruise around town. A high-performance car was the key to instant popularity. So all of us tried to outdo each other with big engines, loud pipes, and big tires. On weekends we raced them, and during the week we put a lot of money and time into maintaining them.

A friend of mine put every dime he had into his high-performance car, and he did an unusual thing to attract attention to himself. He disconnected the brake lines to his rear wheels and put extra-heavy-duty brake pads on his front wheels. He would wait in the high school parking lot until noon hour when all the students would gather around for drag races and other meaningful activities. Then he would put the car in first gear, rev up the engine, and push his foot almost to the floor. The thing would be screaming, making all sorts of noise. Next he would pop the clutch, jam his left foot on the brake pedal, and push the accelerator to the floor.

This created an amazing phenomenon. The back tires would spin like crazy, smoke would pour out of the rear wheel wells, and the front tires would be locked. He would travel at about five miles per hour around the parking lot with the whole car jumping up and down, sputtering and smoking. The front tires smoked because they were skidding and the back ones smoked because they were spinning. He was so cool! We all wanted to do it. He'd vibrate all around the parking lot like that and everybody would clap, thinking it was great.

One day he started his performance with the usual big crowd gathered around. He revved the engine, popped the clutch, and jammed on the brakes. As usual, the car started hopping and vibrating and smoking. But he had done it one too many times. The stress was too much for the car. There was so much tension on the drivetrain that the drive shaft disintegrated and began to bounce across the parking lot. Sparks flew! Parts started falling all over the ground. He nearly destroyed the undercarriage of his car.

Some singles do essentially the same thing. They go beyond kissing and hugging and get themselves sexually aroused. Their minds are racing and their bodies are screaming for additional stimulation. But they remember God's prohibition, so while the gas pedal is all the way to the floor, they slam on the brakes. It's no wonder they experience a high level of sexual frustration.

Our society has many types of singles, but most of them fall into three general categories: the swinging single; those single by circumstance; and the steadfast, spiritual single.

The Swinging Single
We identify the swinging single males by their blown-dry hair, open shirt, hairy chest, sports car with a sunroof, an apartment or condo with a pool and a clubhouse, a water

bed, cable TV with HBO, a fireplace, and mirrors. They walk with an air of confidence, wink at appropriate people at appropriate times, carry embossed business cards with home phone numbers on them, and they wine, dine, dance, and sleep with as many women as they can.

Swinging single women have slender figures, wear Flashdance blouses, carry a copy of Jane Fonda's workout book to work, and eat Dannon yogurt for lunch. They pursue careers, preferably in management, and decide not to have children. They join a health club or two, attend aerobics classes at least twice a week, and frequent tanning salons. They too walk with an air of confidence, live in an apartment or condo with a swimming pool, and drive sports cars. But most important, they know how to turn men's heads with the way they dress, dine, and dance. And, if they intend to play the part very long, they learn to remain elusive and mysterious.

Single by Circumstance

At the middle of the singles spectrum we find the largest segment of the single populace. I call them singles by circumstance. They would rather be married, but for various reasons they're single. Many of them would say, "I would love to be married, but I haven't met the right person yet. I'll stay single until I do." Some are widowed. And others are recovering from divorce. In that broad segment of people who are single by circumstance, some question whether or not they want to ever give up their independence. They know what marriage involves. Others question whether or not they should take the risk of marriage, given the current trends in divorce rates. So they're moving ahead very soberly, very cautiously.

Steadfast, Spiritual Singles

At the other end of the single spectrum are steadfast, spiritual singles. We don't find many of these around.

They're the type Jesus mentioned in Matthew 19:12 and the type Paul talked about in 1 Corinthians 7. These Christian singles have thought about their singleness, prayed about it, discussed it openly with spiritual leaders, and have concluded that remaining single is exactly what God has for them—probably for the rest of their lives.

They are satisfied with their singleness. They have what Jesus referred to as the gift of singleness. It's not for every single, but it's for some. They are so at peace with their singleness that they are completely free to worship God, to serve others, and to advance the kingdom. They don't have divided devotion. They enjoy being with people of the opposite sex, but they are not wired to explode. They're not speeding down a street called Desire with sexual time bombs strapped to their underwear, feeling tense and frustrated over their singleness. Steadfast, spiritual singles, though few in number, are well-adjusted, mature, contented people. They're grateful for the ability to serve God unencumbered and undistracted.

Categories, of course, tend to be cut-and-dried. A good many singles fall somewhere in between these lines. For example, there are many spiritual singles who prefer to be married but have not found the right person yet. They have determined that, until such time when they might have an opportunity to enter into a marriage, they will use their freedom to serve God without distraction. There are many differences between singles. But they all share at least one commonality: they are all sexual. And this is where the tension arises. How can God, who created us as sexual beings, expect singles to live in sexual purity in the middle of a sex-crazed culture?

One thing is sure. God wants everyone, including singles, to live in sexual purity. And He clearly outlines His will with regard to the expression of our human sexuality. His Word clearly reveals that a man and a woman can and should express themselves sexually without guilt or shame, without reservation or inhibition, provided that it happens within the context of marriage. Permanent, monogamous marriage.

And that's it. As harsh as it may seem, the Bible makes it clear. Sexual intercourse outside the bond of marriage is sin. For a married person, it is called adultery. For a single person, the sin is known as fornication. Hebrews 13:4 says, "Fornicators and adulterers God will judge."

This prohibition is listed five times directly and twenty-three times indirectly in the New Testament. I'm stressing it because I hear a steady stream of misinformation about this issue. I talk with singles who pat themselves on the back because they don't involve themselves sexually with married people. They think they're obeying God's will, God's laws. They forget, ignore, or don't know that the Bible also prohibits fornication, which is any sexual intercourse between nonmarried people.

God's Word gives us a third important sexual prohibition that's more general in nature: Steer away from any kind of sexual impurity. Paul mentions it in his letters to the Christians at Colosse and Thessalonica. "Have nothing to do with sexual sin, impurity, lust, and shameful desires" (Col. 3:5, TLB). "Keep clear of sexual sin so that each of you will marry in holiness and in honor—not in lustful passion as the heathen do" (1 Thes. 4:3-5, TLB).

Most Bible scholars believe that this is a clear reference to sexual involvement short of actual intercourse. Or, as it is commonly referred to in our culture, petting—all sexual activity from caressing up to the point of sexual intercourse.

I've heard people say, "I know I can't have intercourse with another person, but everything up to that point is fine. It's not forbidden scripturally." These passages and others take exception to that type of thinking.

Most professional counselors point out that there are

various stages in sexual involvement among people who are dating. The first stage is holding hands, kissing, and embracing. No counselor I know, Christian or secular, would call this sexual sin. It's natural; it's necessary; it's the way we express love and affection to the people we're dating.

The second stage, which I'll refer to as light petting, involves touching and caressing parts of the body while fully clothed. This is where the danger starts. Bodies begin to cry out for additional stimulation. Once people get involved in light petting, they rarely stop there. They usually move to the third stage, heavy petting, which involves genital stimulation and usually leads to climax.

I don't know of a single Christian leader or counselor who would argue that heavy petting is a healthy, positive, God-glorifying activity. In fact, single people who walk with the Lord tell me that both light and heavy petting cause guilt. They say they just don't feel right before God. They sense that they've transgressed a boundary, that they're involved in something God isn't completely pleased with. And not only does it cause guilt, but it also causes an unbelievable amount of frustration. Sexual frustration. And that's easy to explain. Petting causes frustration because it stimulates our God-given sexual design.

According to the way God created us, sexual activity is supposed to lead to merging—to intercourse and release. So starting the process then stopping it short does to our minds and bodies what my friend did to his car.

So what is the alternative? How can we avoid this frustration? There is only one way that I know. Take your foot off the accelerator. Go back to the first stage. More and more Christian counselors are recommending that singles draw the line there. They have seen too many couples learn the hard way what happens when they don't.

Most young singles drastically underestimate the strength of the sexual drive. They find out too late what can happen if they don't keep it under control. Whenever I counsel couples—young, middle-aged, or older—I advise them to stay at the first stage of sexual activity. That is the only way I know to stay free from guilt and free from sexual frustration.

Nothing I've mentioned up to this point is very surprising. We all have a pretty good idea that God's Word prohibits adultery, fornication, and sexual sin. But sometimes we forget the reason. We seem to think that God sat in heaven and rolled dice to decide what we could and couldn't do. And the roll always went against the fun things. But God's standards are not arbitrary. He created what was best for us, and His guidelines are to help us get the most enjoyment from it.

But I seldom, if ever, hear anyone say, "Thank You, Lord, for giving us clear instructions on our sexuality. Thank You for Your wonderful boundaries that You outlined for our enjoyment and protection."

A more typical response is one of resentment. And maybe that's not a strong enough word. Outrage probably describes it better. "It's unfair," they cry. "God is a cosmic killjoy. He creates us to be sexual creatures and arbitrarily decides on a lazy afternoon in glory that half of the population must live in sexual frustration and the other half gets a blank check."

A new believer said to me (and I sensed he was only half kidding), "As I see it, God only had one bad idea. Chastity for singles. Bad idea."

Many singles express their resentment toward God's prohibitions by simply rebelling. They say, "I'll live as I please. I'll sleep with whomever I please, whenever I please. My style is not going to be cramped by an antiquated set of do's and don'ts." So they thumb their noses at God and mistakenly conclude that their way is better than God's and that their wisdom is deeper than His.

But before long complications arise. We cannot break God's laws without suffering the consequences.

I am talking particularly about sexual laws, but we can't break *any* of God's Laws without adverse consequences. We are responsible people with a free will to decide to go God's way or our own. God says that if we go His way, we will be "like a tree firmly planted by streams of water, which yields its fruit in its season, and its leaf does not wither; and in whatever he does, he prospers" (Ps. 1:3). But that is not true of the wicked. "They are like chaff which the wind drives away" (Ps. 1:4). People who go their own way pay a price, the price of disobedience.

Emotional Consequences

We see the consequences of sexual sin all around us. I recently received a phone call from a desperate man. My secretary answered the phone. "Bill," she said, "this person is on the edge. Please talk to him." I took the call, and the man began to describe to me in quivering tones his intense love for a woman. "You have no idea how much I love her," he said.

He told me how they met, how they built trust, and how he communicated with her like no one else he had ever met. He described in detail the first night they made love and how tender it was. They started living together and it was wonderful. But then, with his voice breaking, he said, "And now, oh God, I can hardly stand it; now she has left me and she's sleeping with somebody else."

This man was devastated, absolutely demolished. "I don't want to go on," he said. "I've contemplated suicide. I have never been so hurt and wiped out in my life."

He didn't think there would be any emotional consequences for his sexual sin. He thought he could jump in and out of the sack with no traumatic emotional consequences. But he found out. He was crushed.

I see a steady stream of people who couldn't see God's wisdom regarding sexual prohibitions until they were devastated emotionally. And then they say, "If I'd only known." But no one, not even God, could tell them anything until it was too late.

A woman said recently, "Bill, I dated this man for two years and I finally gave in to his persistence. I gave all of myself to him. And I wanted to. I wanted to show him how much I loved him, so I gave him all of myself. And now he's dating and sleeping with my best friend. Do you know how that makes me feel?"

Yes, I knew how she must feel. Her self-esteem had been demolished. She had been used. Betrayed. Ripped off. I told her that God knows how we feel when that happens, and He's the one who wants to spare us from that. His wisdom and purpose in restricting sexual activity to a permanent, monogamous marriage context is to avoid all of this emotional trauma—to keep people from getting run over and used and abused and betrayed.

Spiritual Consequences

Did you ever go to church on Sunday and feel horrible, dirty? You didn't want to sing and you couldn't pray because of your wild living over the weekend. Have you ever gone to a Wednesday night communion service and listened to a sermon about examining your life and being worthy and pure before God, but all you could think about was what happened the night before?

Some people have lived with spiritual guilt for so long they don't know what a clear conscience is like. They don't remember the last time they stood clean before God, before the person they are dating, or before a communion table. They know what the psalmist meant when he said, "If I had cherished iniquity in my heart, the Lord would not have listened" (Ps. 66:18, RSV). Some have not had a vital prayer life in ages. Their prayers won't go higher than the ceiling because God refuses to hear prayer from people who live in disobedience.

If you have no joy in your spiritual life, no power, it may be because of disobedience. If you feel that God isn't using you, perhaps it's because His plans contradict yours. God doesn't want us to live in fear. He doesn't want us to live in a cloud of guilt. He wants us to be free. He wants each of us to have a clean conscience.

Relational Consequences
In marriage counseling I have found couples who have had trouble dealing with sexual sin prior to marriage. A man said to me, "I committed a lot of sexual sins before I was married and I know my wife did too. She slept around a lot before we were married, and we slept together before we were married. And now that we're married, I don't know if I can trust her to be faithful to me. If she didn't obey any of God's laws before we were married, what's to give me the confidence that she's going to start obeying them now?"

Sexual disobedience has lots of subtle ramifications, and loss of trust and credibility are only two of them.

Physical Consequences
Everywhere, we see the physical consequences of sexual sin. Though it has been labeled sexual freedom, bondage and pain has been the result. The epidemic levels of herpes, gonorrhea, and other forms of venereal disease, as well as the killer AIDS virus, all attest to what God has said all along: Sexual freedom can occur only in the single bond of marriage.

But there is worse news. Those who practice sexual sin are justly getting what they deserve. But there are innocents involved. According to *Newsweek* magazine, having babies is no longer the happy experience it used to be. "There was once a cheerful and widespread belief that when the doctor uttered the familiar words, 'You're pregnant,' most American women wept for joy. No more. Current figures reveal that more than half of the approximately 6 million pregnancies that take place each year in the United States are unintended pregnancies. One point six million of those pregnancies are terminated" (Alan Guttmacher Institute, 1988).

According to a survey conducted by the Centers for Disease Control, nearly 75 percent of the pregnancies which were aborted in a year were those of single women. What a tragedy. In that kind of light, we begin to see the irony of what society calls "free love."

SEVEN

The Abortion Issue

"If a man will begin with certainties, he shall end in doubts; but if he will be content to begin with doubts he shall end in certainties" (Francis Bacon).

The subject of abortion is one of the hottest, most fiercely debated issues in our country. And a lot of "certainty" surrounds it.

On the contrary, my thoughts on abortion began with doubt. I could see both sides of the issue. Perhaps you have been embarrassed, perhaps even looked down on or criticized, because you have some ambiguity about the best response to the problem of unwanted pregnancies. Perhaps the issue doesn't look as black and white to you as it does to your family or friends.

I have to admit that more than a little doubt cast its shadows on my mind for many years. I have come very slowly and painstakingly to my current position on the abortion issue. Part of what made it so difficult for me to deal with was that I felt people on both sides were trying to treat an excruciatingly painful dilemma with compassion.

The pro-choice people told me about Norma, a thirty-nine-year-old mother of five children. She was finally able to work outside the home because her youngest had entered first grade. She and her husband, Sam, had been feeling a lot of tension. The house was too small, but it was all they could afford. Sam thought he'd be much further ahead by the time he reached forty years old, but he'd had to postpone most of his short-term goals because of the kids. Now that Norma could work outside the home, they saw light at the end of the long, dark tunnel.

But for Sam and Norma the light turned out to be a freight train. Norma found out she was pregnant. Sam was furious. Norma was angry with herself. They were both utterly discouraged. Norma couldn't bear the thought of starting over again for the sixth time. Besides that, the family would lose her badly needed income just when they thought they could finally put some of it into a savings account for college tuition.

What would you say to Norma if she came to you for advice? Look closely at her. Can you see her anguish? Can you feel her frustration? Can you sense the pressure she's under? You know you can take her to the clinic in the shopping center down the street and in forty-five minutes Norma's crisis will be over. The family will be able to get on with life as planned. Without question that would take the pressure off Norma and Sam. And it would give their five children a better start in life.

But before you take Norma to the clinic, collect your thoughts. Think of her developing baby. It's more than just a "product" of conception, more than just a mass of tissue. If protected, an infant will poke his head into the world in a few months, look into his parents' eyes, nurse at his mother's breast, and make little noises that will reduce mature parents to sniveling, slobbering, picture-showing baby fanatics. Later, he will laugh and cry and walk and talk and grow. By that time, almost without exception, both parents would gladly offer up their own lives for his if called on to make a decision like that.

All that will happen if the developing baby is protected and allowed to become the full expression of what it is becoming—a human being. No matter how untimely this pregnancy seems, it wasn't the baby's fault.

Few of us would deny a developing baby the opportunity we all had. Someone gave us a place on the human landscape, and most of us are glad about it. Most of us would counsel Norma to give her baby an opportunity to live. We would say, "Norma, I know it's untimely. I know it's going to be difficult, but let the baby live. It wasn't the baby's fault."

I started developing my personal conviction on this issue by trying to look carefully at why pro-choice decisions were being made and why pro-life decisions were being made. I tried to determine what values determined each of those choices.

Surprisingly, I often found that the operative value in both choices was compassion. Women were counseled to get abortions out of compassion. Women were counseled not to get abortions out of compassion. Everybody was being compassionate. But who was being right?

I needed to find some guidelines to determine who was right. I needed more than compassion for a standard. It took me a long time to work through all the factors that influence abortion decisions, but after a long, difficult, soul-searching journey, I found myself in the center of the camp of those who strongly seek to protect the lives of unborn children. Putting it another way, I find abortion to be an unacceptable alternative to the problem of unwanted pregnancies.

The Bible

The first place I looked for guidelines was the Bible. Even though the Bible doesn't contain concise antiabortion clauses that we can paint on picket signs, it is full of divine directions that speak to the issues surrounding abortion.

First, the Bible clearly indicates that the sovereign God is at work in the lives of human beings from conception, all during life in the womb, during childbirth, through infancy, into adulthood and, at least with His own children, all through eternity.

Second, the Bible reveals that human beings alone, distinct from all other forms of creation, are created in the image of God.

One of the implications of being made in the image of God is that human life has an extremely high value attached to it. It's different from animal life. It is not expendable. God gave much attention in both the Old and New Testaments to protecting human life from becoming trivial or profane. He gave laws to protect human beings from violence and oppression. And this law from the Big Ten protects us from murder: Thou Shalt Not Kill. God has not given us the prerogative to end human life. We cannot create life, and we have no right to end it.

Throughout the whole Old Testament, because human beings are made in the image of God, we are taught to respect life, to preserve it, to honor it. In the New Testament, we see that Jesus' words reverberate throughout His teachings and throughout history as He instructs His followers to do some very radical things, such as love their enemies.

He also told them to turn the other cheek when they were wronged instead of figuring out how to strike back. Then Jesus said He wanted His people to defend, care for, and provide assistance to the defenseless members of society—people without political power, forgotten people, people with no voice to speak for themselves. Jesus wants us to speak for those who have no voice, to defend those who cannot defend themselves, to use our power and influence to protect the poor, the widows and orphans, the handicapped, the oppressed, and the children.

While studying abortion, I kept asking myself, "Who are the most vulnerable and defenseless people in our society? Who has no voice, no vote, and no political power base?"

The answer: Developing children. They are totally helpless. Unlike newborns, they cannot even breathe on their own. Jesus said that when we defend and care for the least of these, we have done it unto Him (Matt. 25:40).

For the last fifteen years I have attempted to be a serious student of the Word of God. I have a lot more to learn, but the more I read this Book and the more I study it and the more I expose my value system to it, the stronger I feel about protecting unborn babies. The value of human life is one reason. Jesus' commandments to protect human beings from violence is another reason. And at the top of the list is my increased wonderment at the fact that Jesus gave His own life to redeem human beings. What more could He say about the value of human life?

Medical Information
The Bible wasn't the only source of information that influenced my decision to join those who oppose abortion. The second influence was recent medical data pertaining to the issue of unwanted pregnancies. I have begun to see a marked change in the medical community's posture on abortion. Because of the rapid technological advances in medical equipment and in the field of fetology, there is a lot more prebirth information to deal with than ever before.

Twenty years ago, neither the mother nor even some members of the medical community knew exactly what they were dealing with when a woman miscarried. Products of conception were being expelled from wombs routinely. But a veil of mystery covered the whole matter.

The days of mystery, the days of wondering, are coming to a close, however. The veil is being raised because members of the medical teams know what they're dealing with. And that has caused more than a little stir.

Most of us know what a fetus looks like at twelve weeks. We've seen pictures in books, magazines, on television, or in doctor's offices that have been taken in vitro by means of some new method of technology. A three-month-old fetus is not a mass of tissue. Some of you may have been as shocked as I was to see a fetus that small with facial features, moving arms and legs, and a thumb stuck in its mouth. You thought what I thought: "That's a baby! Who's calling that a tissue mass? It's a whole lot more than that."

Doctors and researchers from universities and hospitals, including Harvard Medical School and Mayo Clinic, who have no biblical or Christian bias, have reported finding evidence that supports the pro-life position. A growing number of researchers are saying that when the egg and sperm combine to form the zygote (i.e., the moment of conception), we are dealing with a developing human being.

They are saying that there is no other decisive moment during pregnancy when the status of human being is conferred on a fetus. From conception on, we're dealing with a human being.

U.S. Surgeon General C. Everett Koop in his book *The Right to Live, The Right to Die* (Tyndale) poses these questions: "Would you go into a nursery and kill a week-old baby? How about a one-day-old baby? An hour-old baby? How about an hour before delivery? Or a day before delivery? A week before delivery? Three weeks before delivery?" The Surgeon General argues dramatically that there is no line of demarcation that delineates when a baby changes from a subhuman tissue mass to a living human being.

My wife had two miscarriages. The second was a set of twins, and her pregnancy ended at about four months. Rather naively, but with a certain amount of curiosity motivating me, I asked the doctor if I could go to the lab and see the fetuses.

"Well, it's kind of an unusual request," he said, "but if you'd like to, come with me."

So I went. And what I saw was a lot more than tissue masses. I could see very clearly that they were both boys, and I could identify their arms, legs, toes, fingers, eyes, and noses. Definitely not blobs of tissue.

Research indicates that 80 to 85 percent of women seeking abortions change their minds if they see pictures of developing babies approximately the same age as the fetuses they're carrying.

I have been surprised by how many doctors are changing to an antiabortion position on medical grounds. Not on moral or spiritual grounds. They are realizing that fetuses are more than mere tissue masses.

Counseling Experiences
The counseling I have done with women who have had abortions is the final source of information that helped shape my thinking on this subject. These experiences do not have the authority of Scripture nor the credibility of scientific research, but they have influenced me.

I've been told by some that the majority of women who have had one abortion or more are not fazed a bit by it, that it's like having a wisdom tooth pulled. No big deal. I've been told that repeatedly, so maybe it's true. But I keep asking myself why I have never met even one such woman. During my years in ministry, I've counseled hundreds of women, not all Christians, who have had abortions, and I have never talked with one who wasn't wounded deeply because of it.

John 16:8 says the Holy Spirit is going to convict the world of sin. The Holy Spirit has a universal ministry of giving human beings a sense of right and wrong.

I keep meeting women and receiving mail and phone calls from women who tell me how abortion has scarred their lives. One woman wrote: "Bill, I'm sure my letter won't be any different from the hundreds that you receive concerning this subject, but knowing others have experienced this doesn't lessen my pain. My hands are shaking as I write this letter and my eyes are filling with tears again. I too made a terrible mistake some years ago. I had an abortion, and I wish to God I hadn't."

One woman said, "Words can't describe how terrible I feel. Ashamed, dirty, and guilty. Oh, the guilt you will never understand. I was wrongfully led to believe that an abortion was the only answer to my unwanted pregnancy and now I am so angry I can hardly stand it."

Another said, "I walked out of the clinic looking the same on the outside, but no one saw the damage and the pain I have experienced on the inside. I still feel it almost every day. Please tell women not to believe that abortion is a quick fix. It is not a quick fix; it is far from it."

After all these years of this kind of input, something tells me that an abortion is different from having a wisdom tooth pulled. Even if I had no biblical or medical basis, I would counsel against abortion because of the resulting psychological disturbances I have seen.

Although my personal position on abortion is firm, I still respect people on the other side. I don't agree with them, but I don't think they are categorically wicked. I think they're uninformed biblically, medically, and probably psychologically.

If you are still undecided on this issue or perhaps even pro-choice or pro-abortion, please do some additional homework. Search the Scriptures, read the most recent medical data, talk to women who have had abortions. Study, think, read, pray, act, ask questions. Don't be swept along by the quick fix, convenience-store mentality that permeates our culture.

If you have already come to an antiabortion position, I challenge you to follow the leading of the Holy Spirit. If He should direct you to write letters, march, picket, or rally to stop what's going on, follow His leading. Become as involved as the Spirit of God leads you to become, but don't become overzealous. Do not call pro-choice people names like baby-killers. Rhetoric like that is not productive.

If you are militantly pro-life, I urge you to be as concerned about other issues that threaten the quality of human life that already exists. Be as concerned about those as you are about abortion. Be concerned about poverty, hunger, disease, and war. If you are truly pro-life you will be concerned about those issues as well. Be activists, but with integrity and compassion. And without violence.

If you are a pregnant woman facing the decision right now, don't believe those who call abortion a quick fix. Call a counselor. Talk to your pastor or a trusted Christian friend. There are better options. Thousands of Christian couples would love to raise your child. A couple wrote to ask me to plead with pregnant women in our church not to abort. Another couple said, "We've been waiting for six years. We'll raise the child in a Christian home."

EIGHT
The Pornography Problem

We live in a world of cheap, quick thrills. You can get a quarter-pounder in less than two minutes, guaranteed. Sit on the couch and with the punch of a remote, turn on music, or the tube, or the VCR. Take a pill and, within minutes, clear out your sinuses, settle your stomach, or lose your appetite. It's all so simple. Partake and dispose. A thrill or a cure a minute.

The same thing is happening in our sex-crazed world. We want our pleasure cheap and quick with no strings attached. Abortion is a gruesome example of our throwaway society. If something is unwanted or unexpected, including a sacred human life, our inclination is to get rid of the problem instead of dealing with it.

Pornography is another example of our throwaway mentality. For less than the price of a steak dinner, we can feast our lust on sexual images. Quick and easy. And when the pages get worn, we simply make another trip to the convenience store or the video outlet. Sexual fulfillment for $4.95. But what comes neatly packaged in those glossy pages or technicolor frames is pure deception. Consider the following letter written by a man who regularly worships at Willow Creek Community Church:

> I'm thirty-four years old and I can tell you truthfully,
> I was in bondage to desire for twenty-five of my
> thirty-four years. Most specifically in the area of por-
> nography. It was an addiction as powerful and as
> seductive as any deadly drug, only slower and more
> subtle in its effect. It all started when I was six years
> old and I would sneak peeks at our neighbor's *Play-
> boy* magazines. I became enamored with the female
> anatomy so much that I used to cut out advertise-
> ments from traditional magazines and carry them
> with me. The adults in my life thought it was cute
> and funny that I had the desire to look at pictures of
> nude women at six years old. It was just further
> evidence that I was all boy. This seemingly innocent
> practice continued for several years, relatively un-
> changed and unchallenged by my parents. But ev-
> erything changed dramatically when I was twelve
> years old and I discovered sexual self-stimulation.
> That's considered a natural progression in the sexual
> awakening that accompanies puberty, but in my
> case it was like going from cigarettes to heroin. This
> new practice actually allowed me to fulfill a physical
> act with euphoric results. I was now in total control.
> In my fantasies I picked which girl or girls I would
> be with. While in junior high school, my thoughts
> were primarily on girls, not schoolwork, and I
> would focus my attention on my female teachers;
> they were closer in age and build to the women in
> my magazines. Even though I had some clumsy sex-
> ual experiences early on, they were, frankly, disap-
> pointing compared to my sexual fantasy life. Espe-
> cially when the acceptable sex magazines like *Playboy*
> and *Penthouse* became more explicit.
>   In my mid-teens I was no longer just looking at

pictures. I began to read "Playboy Advisor" and "Penthouse Letters." They helped me to develop what I call my fornication philosophy. Because of what I saw and read in these sex magazines, and because of a new permissiveness in movies and society in general, I felt not only justified in my own philosophy, but the world around me was confirming my sexual wisdom. I was fifteen years old. At the age of sixteen I met the girl who would become my wife. She was the most beautiful girl I had ever known. She had the physical attributes that I had grown to adore. She was a year and a half older than me. It was love at first sight for both of us, and the combination of her beauty and her unselfish love kept me from diving headfirst into the sexual underworld. However, even though we enjoyed lovemaking with daily frequency at sixteen, my appetite only grew more and more insatiable. After a couple of years of marriage, I became obsessed with the need to act out what I considered spontaneous and exciting public elevator-type experiences that were so common in the 'Penthouse Letters.' When those desires went unfulfilled, I turned to X-rated movies and films to supplement my magazine habit. My mind was so filled with these images that even when I was making love to my wife, my thoughts were continually flooded with other images.

After a while I found myself in the X-rated movie arcades occupying private booths, looking at images on film, vicariously participating in sexual acts that would never be fulfilled at home. I started to become unsatisfied at home; began putting enormous pressures on my wife to either grow with me sexually or I would leave her. My threats constantly hung over her head. Somehow, she managed to hang in there despite my sickness. She put up with my maintain-

ing a sex magazine collection that was large enough
to require cataloging. The images that were etched
into my mind from ages six to twelve were so strong
that I went back and paid top dollar for vintage back
issues just to relive those early thrills. Not only was I
putting heavy sexual demands on my wife, but I
also had several hundred magazine mistresses to
satisfy me, along with regular trips to the video arcades just to keep my interest up. But nothing satisfied me sexually, nothing.

About a year after our first child was born and
after several divorce threats, I read a book which led
me to Jesus. Once I came to the Lord, my sin was
revealed to me. I genuinely wanted to clean up my
act, but I knew that after twenty years of addiction I
couldn't go cold turkey. I knew that I was not strong
enough to do that, but I figured if God wanted me
to, He would provide me with the strength eventually. God began to work with me by softening my
heart, opening my eyes to the wonderful gifts He
had provided for me—my wife and my child. After
five years of prayer and many miracles, I was given
the strength to throw away my previously prized
magazine collection. This was the beginning of complete deliverance from this addiction. Over the next
few years I was finally able to stop visiting the X-
rated arcades; ultimately, after twenty continuous
years of habitual self-stimulation, I was able to stop.
The Lord has helped me and made our marriage
now what it was meant to be. Praise God for His
miraculous work! He is faithful!

That man is a truly born-again believer who has fought
a fierce battle against pornography. But isn't he the exception? Aren't we making too much hoopla over pornography? I have hundreds of concerns more pressing

than taking *Playboy* magazines out of the hands of those
who buy them occasionally to read articles by famous
people, even Presidents. Besides, if I remember correctly,
I viewed some of the airbrushed beauties on the
centerfolds of some of those magazines when I was in
junior and senior high school. It didn't ruin my life. You
don't find me wearing a trench coat and hanging around
school yards. I'm happily married with two wonderful
children.

In the past few years, I have heard the cries of people
claiming that pornography is proliferating in the news-
stands and convenience stores in this country and that
we should do something to stop it. I hear the urgency in
their voices. I keep up with university studies on this
issue, the Attorney General's commissions, suggested
boycotts, pickets, letter-writing campaigns, and the like.
Area leaders even contacted me some time ago to help
them close down the adult bookstores in our community.
And all along I have found myself asking, What is the big
deal? Why all the drama?

The big deal is that pornography has changed. It
changed without my realizing it, and my guess is that
most other Christians don't realize it either. I had one of
the rudest awakenings of my life when I researched this
subject.

Part of the motivation for this study came out of a
lunch I had with James Dobson. He had just finished
serving on the Attorney General's Commission on Pornography. After lunch, he asked me what I was doing
about the pornography problem facing our country.

"Well," I said, "I'm intending to do a message on it in
the fall."

"How are you going to prepare for it?" he asked.

"Well, I haven't really determined that yet."

He looked me right in the eye and said, "Get yourself
educated, young man, firsthand. Get educated and then

just do as God leads from that point on."

So I did. And I have to confess, with a certain amount of embarrassment, that when I began my study a little voice told me that this might even be interesting. After all, I'm as red-blooded as the next guy. But it wasn't interesting. It was disgusting and depressing and filthy. It was shocking and sickening. Pornography has changed.

First, I got copies of pornographic magazines, and I found out that the kind I used to sneak peeks at in high school doesn't even exist anymore. I couldn't locate one magazine with partially clad women—the mild kind of pornography that was the standard fifteen years ago. Instead, I learned that today's mild form of pornography— the stuff that we can buy in area convenience stores— contains photo layouts that almost defy the imagination, including pictures of women being bound and gagged, raped, whipped, and abused. Standard fare includes an array of multiple sexual partners in heterosexual, homosexual, and lesbian photo poses. The underlying theme is usually domination or violence. The rougher magazines depict gang rape scenes, torture scenes, and bestiality. Some of the most popular magazines show men and women having sexual relationships with children ranging in age from three to eight years old. I was appalled and outraged. And then I learned that there are 240 million pornographic magazines printed each year in this country.

Next, I had my assistants rent some adult videos. I'm not sure what I was expecting, but I saw a steady stream of sexual perversion, including fathers having sex with daughters, sons with mothers, siblings with each other, adults with children, and children with children. And sales of these adult videos are going off the charts.

And then I learned about the seedier side of the pornography industry—the adult bookstores. There are more adult bookstores in this country than there are Mc-Donald's hamburger restaurants. We have more than 20,000 adult bookstores in the United States. They sell sex magazine and sexual paraphernalia, but their major attraction is the film booths. This is where patrons pump quarters into coin boxes and view pornographic movies that defy description. And what goes on in those booths defies description. A police officer in my church infiltrated these bookstores and told me things not fit to print.

There is also the hi-tech side of the pornography industry. Dial-a-Porn allows callers to listen to a tape recording of a woman making erotic conversation and erotic sounds. Hundreds of thousands of calls are made every day to Dial-a-Porn, and kids at junior high schools pass around the numbers to one another.

Computer sex is also available now. Subscribers hook into the network and pornography comes to their television screens via the phone lines.

Pornography is a $6–8 billion-a-year industry. Most of it is controlled by organized crime, almost all of it going untouched, and it's growing exponentially. Pornography isn't anything like it was ten or fifteen years ago. It has degenerated into the pits of depravity.

But what concerns me most is the damage pornography does to the people who get caught up in it.

Pornography Is Addicting

People don't understand. When we indulge our sexual appetite and get into explicit videos, movies, and magazines, we find that pornography is addicting. It pushes us further and further. It makes us want more, more, more. Like alcohol and drugs, an addiction to pornography shatters lives. I received a letter recently from someone in my church who is struggling with this problem. He wrote: "I am an emotional invalid. I am crippled by my addiction to pornography. It paralyzes my spiritual life, it perverts my view of the world, it distorts my social life, it wreaks havoc in my emotional stability, it renders me useless and destroys any possibility of God using me, and I just can't stop. . . . Lust eats me up, yet it doesn't satisfy. Pornography simply intensifies the problem. It promises me everything, it produces nothing, and I just can't seem to stop using it."

Pornography isn't physiologically addictive, but it can and often does become psychologically addictive. It's important for us to realize that sexuality has a progressive nature. It takes more and more to satisfy our desire. Early in our dating experiences, holding hands gave us an enormous thrill. But after a while that became mundane, so we worked up to the next thrill, perhaps an embrace, and then the next, maybe some kissing.

What gave a thrill yesterday isn't enough today. And pornography works the same way. People who use pornography continually seek something slightly more erotic, a little more bizarre. Over time they develop the same need-fix syndrome that other substance abusers feel. They need a porn fix.

Some time ago, I tried to help a woman whose husband was addicted to pornography. I asked her to chart his behavior so we could narrow down where specific problems might be. She brought in a phone bill of over $300. We learned that he was making twenty to thirty Dial-a-Porn calls per night. He also had a stack of magazines four feet high and boxes full of pornographic films. He was an addict, and it destroyed their marriage.

Those of us who have never been addicted to anything will never understand the intensity of desire that an addict feels. But we must be as careful, as understanding, and as compassionate as we can be because people who matter to God and who sit next to us in church have unintentionally crossed that invisible line. They are enslaved to a pattern of life that leads to heartache and ruin, and they don't know how to stop.

Once addiction sets in, it's an almost sure road to ruin, unless something happens to stop the downward spiral.

Pornography Assaults the Dignity of Women

Showing women being seduced, stripped, and handled like farm animals is an obvious and hideous assault on their dignity. It is especially vulgar and disgusting to Christians because Jesus made it a point to right some of the wrongs that had been perpetrated against women in His day. One of His missions was to elevate the role and dignity of women, to let them know that they were full image-bearers, that they had gifts, talents, and abilities, and that they were not second-class citizens. So Christians should be disgusted when they see a woman's dignity assaulted in pornographic material.

But what I became much more concerned about during my research was pornography's subtle assault on the nature and character of women. Pornography depicts women as having an insatiable appetite for sex. The magazines and the videos convince men that women everywhere are walking around twenty-four hours a day craving their next sexual encounter. That not only assaults the dignity of women by reducing them to the level of animals in heat, but it also feeds a dangerous kind of thought process in men's minds.

The constant presence of the rape myth in today's pornographic material frightens me. If there is a single common thread that ties pornographic content together, it is the continual emphasis, made in dozens of ways, that even though women indicate they are not interested in a man's sexual advances, really they are. The theme is rampant in magazines and videos. A man will begin a sexual encounter with a woman. She isn't the least bit interested; in fact, she is visibly repulsed by his advances. This motivates the man because he knows that deep down she is craving a sexual experience. So the man persists and begins to force himself on the woman. After an exciting struggle, the woman is overcome by the strength of the man, and as the actual sexual encounter is happening she not only stops fighting off the man but she pleads for him to continue and ends up begging for more.

I have a beautiful wife and a vivacious twelve-year-old daughter, and I'm living with the keen awareness that there are thousands of men in our community who are addicted to pornography, who are wandering around in public places, convinced that all women are craving sex all day. If a woman resists, she really wants him to overpower her and take her forcibly. Then she will enthusiastically participate in sex with him and thank him afterward.

That's a lie from the pit of hell. And pornography feeds men those lies in living color with music in the background. Close-ups, careful lighting, slickly produced films and pictures. But rape is no glamorized production. Rape wounds a woman about as deeply as anything can. It's a hideous crime. And pornography producers and merchants not only keep the rape myth alive, but they spread it. Pornography has changed. And it ought to be stopped.

Pornography Undermines the Physical Relationship in Marriage

Most of us have been led to believe that viewing pornography with our spouses might add a little vitality to a rather routine physical relationship. I know that many married couples in my church routinely view adult videos to add some spice to their sexual lives. Initially, viewing pornography will excite and stimulate marriage partners. No question about it. But it is not the "initially" that I'm concerned about. It is the "eventually" that concerns me.

I counseled with a woman recently who is a leader in another church. Her husband is an elder there. The two of them began using pornography as a marital stimulus some years ago. She came to see me because her marriage is in shambles. Over an extended period of time, the use of pornography will prove to be counterproductive to the development of a physical relationship in marriage, and continued usage usually leads to sexual frustration and sexual dysfunction.

God designed marital sexuality to flow out of the context of a loving and intimate relationship where nurturing, communication, sharing, serving, romancing, and tenderness go on. When those values are cultivated in a marriage, they arouse sexual interest. Sexual intercourse then becomes an expression of caring, of loving, a way of saying to the partner, "You matter to me. I love you and I want to communicate that to you tenderly as we make love together."

The use of pornography short-circuits all of that. It reduces the sexual dimension of marriage to a biologically induced athletic event, and eventually, because of the emphasis on the athletic aspects of the sexual experience, there is no longer much emphasis on the loving part of marriage. Once that is drained out of a relationship, the heart and soul of marital sexuality is gone. The woman starts feeling used and abused, and the man starts feeling frustrated and empty. He begins to think that a new position, a new activity or, better yet, a new partner or partners would relieve his frustration and emptiness.

When sexuality no longer flows out of intimacy, communication, private nurturing, love, and tenderness, expect something serious to happen down the road in your marriage. I've talked with many couples whose physical relationship was destroyed through the extended use of pornography. They naively assumed it would be a stimulant, but now they sit dysfunctional.

A woman told me this week, "My husband and I can't have a sexual experience without pornography to get us started. But then we feel filthy and guilty and empty." Extended use of pornography will undermine the physical relationship in marriage.

Pornography Has a Devastating Impact on Children

Pornography inevitably falls into the hands of children. Most people I know were exposed to some form of pornography before they entered high school. Kids get the magazines. Kids see the videos and watch the cable stations. The use of pornography by young children often leads to misguided sexual experimentation. And the results are shattering to their sexuality. They may require years of professional therapy to readjust.

One woman said that she has spent the last twenty years of her life trying to recover from damage caused by her brother. He began viewing pornography as a twelve-year-old and didn't know where to focus his sexual excitement; so he used his ten-year-old sister. For all these years she has been afflicted with nightmares and sexual confusion because of those early encounters with a brother whose mind was perverted by a magazine.

If pornography distorts the sexual perspective of adults, think what it must do to children who are incapable of making wise decisions about simple things, let alone something as complex as human sexuality.

Children become victims of pornography in another way. They fall prey to the seduction of adults whose use of pornography has awakened in them a sickening interest in the sexual exploitation of young children. A man from my church, in an unsigned letter, admitted that he is addicted to pornography and that he made advances to a twelve-year-old girl.

Producers and merchants of pornography are focusing

their marketing strategy for the next wave of explicit materials on children between the ages of twelve and seventeen. Who's going to stop them?

And there's so much more. A group on the West Coast has this motto: "Sex before eight, before it's too late." There are books on the market today that give careful, explicit instructions to child sexual molesters. These books describe in great detail how to seduce young children into having sexual encounters.

Finding a Way out of Bondage

Husbands who are toying with pornography at home or in other places need to admit their addiction and seek help. Wives who are being pressured by their husbands to view some of these things should stand up and say they're not going to watch. Tell him it will lead down a dead-end road and you don't want to end up there. Though you can't control what he does, you can control what you do.

If you are a light user, an occasional voyeur, a periodic subscriber or renter of porn, I would remind you of 1 Corinthians 10:12: "Therefore let any one who thinks that he stands take heed lest he fall." Anybody who says, "I can experiment and I can handle it," should know that this stuff is highly addictive. Every time you view pornography your concept of the dignity of women and sexuality is subconsciously undermined. And if you're careless with the material it could fall into the hands of a child. My advice to light users is to say no. Throw it away. Forget it. Let your mind dwell on better things. Make a decision to never again pollute your mind with pornography.

If you are a heavy user, addict, or near addict, you feel what is happening to you emotionally, but you probably don't understand what is happening intellectually. That's the way addictions function. You need to read Jerry

Kirk's book, *The Mind Polluters*. It is the best book available for people who want to know about pornography—how to get help or how to get involved in stopping its spread.

If you are involved in pornography, get help. Tell someone about your problem. It's not the kind of thing that heals by itself. We all have areas of sinfulness that we're struggling with, and none of us are any better or any worse than others. We all need the courage to ask for help.

Those who have no personal problem with pornography but who are outraged by its threat to society can join the fight against it. If God leads you, become active in your community. Write letters. Speak to store owners. Picket, boycott, do whatever God leads you to do. You could make a difference.

Our church has a ministry called "Heal." It's an accountability group filled with people who are wrestling with the same kinds of problems. Anyone can walk into that room and say, "I'm a sinner who needs help," and the people in the room will say, "Come on in. That's who we are. We're finding help through accountability, honesty, and fellowship." In these groups we give people the opportunity to come out of the closet and to talk to other Christians who are addicted or having serious problems with this matter.

We do this only under the guidance and careful scrutiny of trained counselors, and we protect people's identities. If your church doesn't have this type of ministry, you might consider starting one. Many people struggling with unhealthy sexual desire could benefit from a program of accountability, honesty, and fellowship. The only way to combat some of these problems is to get them out in the open, break the silence, and break the deadly pattern.

It's easy for me to say, "Don't fill your mind with garbage; don't even get started." But for some people that advice comes too late. Our minds are like vacuums—they're always sucking in dirt. Unlike the Hoover in the closet, sometimes we can't flip the switch when we want to turn it off. We can't always keep our minds from taking things in, but we can control what we take in. The best antidote to pornography is to fill our minds with things that are clean and pure. Philippians 4:8: "Whatever is true, whatever is honorable, whatever is just, whatever is pure, whatever is lovely, whatever is of good repute . . . think about these things."

Some people think that pornography is harmless. They think that they can handle it and not have it affect their behavior. But whatever we put into our minds will eventually find its way out. The chief deception of pornography is that it provides a cheap thrill. It doesn't. It is very costly. It is dehumanizing, degrading, and addictive. Pornography reduces the sex act to an animal act, a mechanical coupling, a "screw." Gone is the intimacy, commitment, and love. It strips away the very things that God designed into sexuality to make it sacred. Once that corrosive process begins, even in our thoughts, it makes us vulnerable to all sorts of perversion.

Sexual Abuse

"We looked on the outside like your everyday family. But behind those doors we were not. My dad started feeling me when I was nine. The reason he did not do it earlier was because he was messing around with my older sister. This went on for four years. My mother knew what was going on. She was told a few times, but she could not face that her husband was messing around with her daughter. My dad would be real nice to me when I would cooperate with him. If I did not cooperate, he would be mean. He would even choke me and say I'd better not say anything to anyone. You see, there was a lot of fear in my life. I figured I could go to the police, but I was scared what my dad would do. And I did not want to break up my parents' marriage, and I did not want people to know what was going on in our home. So I didn't say anything."

This letter and the two following were written to me by women from my church. Obviously, sexual abuse is not a problem that bypasses Christians.

Another woman wrote, "I am a part of a family secret. I played a part in a secret sin. I'm in my twenties now and all this occurred between the time I was seven and eleven, but I still carry the emotional scars. I really don't think those scars will ever leave. You may wonder what this family secret is. Well, my uncle is a child molester and I was his victim. . . . The thing that hurts me the most is that I have always felt like the guilty party, that somehow I could have stopped him. As an adult, and now as a Christian, I know this is just false guilt, but I spent a lot of years in a private torture chamber. I think right now the biggest thing I feel is hurt, a deep, aching hurt that never really goes away. When I was younger I was much angrier, so I had to give it to the Lord. I used to have nightmares; they aren't so frequent anymore, but I'll probably always have some. I never let anybody touch me anywhere. Maybe someday I'll get over that. I get nervous at family parties when everyone is leaving and my uncle steps up to kiss me good-bye."

And another wrote, "The incest I experienced was at the hands of my father whose alcoholism was secondary to his severe mental illness. My mother knew, but was afraid and would not seek help. The only nurturing I ever remember was that of a sexual nature with my father. It must have been too painful for my mother. The only way she knew how to deal with that was simply by not acknowledging my presence at all in our home. That rejection penetrated my heart at a young age, and so I clung to a father who abused me."

These letters were written by a few of the victims who had the courage to admit it and the desire to get well. When I discuss sexual abuse I'm referring to that wide range of sexual overtures that adults make to youngsters: Adults who caress and stroke the bodies of young children. Adults who try to have and occasionally succeed in having intercourse with them. Adults who insist that children perform various sexual acts on them. In short, we're talking about any adult-initiated sexual activity with a young child.

We suburban dwellers tend to think of sexual abuse, molestation, and incest as city problems. But that is not the case. I know of several victims in my one upper-middle-class suburban church.

You might be married to a sexually abused woman and not know anything about it. Your best friend might have been a victim. Your neighbor might be hiding the scars of an abusive past. Sexual abuse is the most secret of all sexual sins, so it is not uncommon to know a victim without knowing anything about his or her past. Sexual abuse does not discriminate. Both males and females have been abused and felt the horrible effects of sexual abuse. (For the purpose of illustration, we will be focusing on sexual abuse of females in this chapter.)

We're living in a sick society. If you read daily newspapers you know how rampant the problem of sexual abuse is. But some may wonder if it is really happening more often today or if we just hear more about it. The statistics are difficult to compile because the majority of victims are afraid to say anything to anyone. They keep their secrets while they're young. Then, because they've developed a pattern of keeping quiet, they often keep their secrets forever. But some statistics are available, and one leading researcher estimates that 40 percent of all women in the United States have had at least one experience of sexual abuse during childhood (David Finkelhor, *Science News*, April 1980). *Psychology Today* (Feb. 1987) reports that "as many as 40 million people, about 1 in 6 Americans, may have been sexually victimized as children."

The Danger

My research on this subject was, in a word, shattering. I had no idea how widespread this problem is. And one realization in particular hit me with the force of a speeding Mack truck: Adultery, immorality, fornication, and homosexuality are, for the most part, conscious choices made by consenting adults, but sexual abuse is different. One of the parties is anything but consenting.

Severe cases of sexual abuse seem to occur in a certain type of home. It seems to be more prevalent in lower-income homes, though not exclusively so. It's much more common in homes with stepfathers, and it's more likely to happen in homes that lack emotional closeness between the mother and daughter. Stepfathers are five times more likely to victimize daughters than biological fathers. Most experiences happen to young girls between the ages of three and thirteen; the average age is seven and a half. Most of the abuse happens in the child's own home when the mother and other family members are absent. And most offenders are direct family members or close friends or relatives. Alcohol and drug usage are frequently involved.

Because sexual abuse is so often a family affair, it is essential, though extremely difficult, for parents to talk to their children about it. Don't think for a minute that it could never happen in your family. Open communication between parents and children is a necessity. Children must feel free to report any instance of questionable conduct.

The Ramifications

The ramifications of sexual abuse are almost too numerous to mention, but the following seven are the ones I believe are the most significant.

The first ramification is hatred toward the offender. This is not a mild dislike. It is a deep hatred that most of us will never know. Some children are abused several times a week for years. Imagine living with that. Imagine the fear and pain of it. Imagine the hopelessness of having no way to stop it. Imagine being threatened with death or a beating if you ever tell anyone. The hatred grows even after the abuse stops. When the victim is older and thinks back on it, she is not only angry at what happened, but angry at what didn't happen. She realizes the positive experiences she should have had in a family. The anger that began against the offender spreads to others, including society in general and God.

The second ramification is mistrust. "I'll never trust another man as long as I live" is a statement I've heard countless times from abused women. This spreads over into relationships with male authority figures.

I have found this to be true in the ministry at my church. Several women who seemed very spiritual and had an obvious desire to grow with the Lord were very critical toward the male elders and toward my ministry in the church. It seemed that every time I gave a message that had any real challenge to it I would sense resistance from these women. As I got to know them better, I asked, "Why is it that you resist me so much? Why don't you trust my leadership?" More than once that broke down a wall, and the truth came out. One woman said, "I have reasoned for many years that if I ever submit to another man, I expose myself to the possibility of abuse. Every time I submitted to my uncle or my father I got abused, and I'm never going to submit to any man, because I make the connection of submission and surrender and cooperation with abuse." For many women, even trusting God and relating to Him as a perfect, loving Father is difficult.

The third ramification is guilt. Even though they were the victims, these women feel shame and guilt. They feel stained. To hear a godly woman who was the innocent victim of sexual abuse say to me in private conversation, "I just feel dirty" breaks my heart. What must it do to God's heart? They live with a false but overpowering sense of guilt.

The fourth ramification of sexual abuse is no self-esteem. The woman reasons, "I'm stained now. I've been abused and mistreated and victimized. I am not worth anything to anyone. Who would want dirty merchandise? Who would want me?"

This problem is different from and more serious than low self-esteem. Many of us suffer from low self-esteem because we're unhappy with our body weight or shape, our job, our talents, or our overall state in life. But low self-esteem is mild compared to the absence of self-esteem. These women feel worthless. And they live in fear that people who find out the truth about them will hate them. So they can't get close to anyone.

The fifth ramification is the diminished desire for sexual activity in marriage. Every touch during those childhood years was like the searing touch of a branding iron. How can victims suddenly change channels and learn to find pleasure in being touched?

The sixth ramification is dependency on drugs and alcohol. Those who have no idea how to put a shattered life back together will try anything to relieve the pain. People who live a twenty-four hour nightmare will try anything to block it out. Relief to many sexually abused people is spelled h-i-g-h.

The seventh ramification is second-generation physical or sexual abuse. A woman abused as a child frequently abuses her own children. This is difficult to document, and the research is somewhat unclear. But there seems to be an indication that women who feel rage, guilt, and worthlessness, and who become dependent on drugs and alcohol, also become extremely volatile. And many times they express that volatility in violence toward misbehaving children.

The Hope
The ramifications of sexual abuse sound overwhelming and are indeed difficult to overcome, but healing is not

out of the question. Sexual abuse of a child by the father can have particularly damaging spiritual consequences. I have counseled several victims who have an immensely difficult time relating to God the Father because of the damage their earthly fathers have done. It can take literally years of healing to regain trust. But wholeness is not outside the realm of possibility.

As I have mentioned in regard to other problem areas, the healing process requires three things: supernatural assistance, support from friends and family, and professional help.

People who have been sexually abused are in desperate need of a supportive and saving relationship with Jesus Christ. He alone has the power to rebuild shattered lives. He can heal you.

If you have been sexually abused and seek healing for your wounds, confiding in Christ is the first step. The second step is confiding in a trusted friend or family member. This is a frightening thing to do because you risk rejection. But you probably will never be free until you tell another person what really happened to you.

Nearly every sexually abused person who has worked up the courage to confide in me has left our conversation soaring. Not because I had any great insights to offer. I rarely have brilliant insights to offer anybody. But I can be a good listener. And so can many others. Don't keep the secret to yourself. Satan will keep whispering to you, "They will laugh at you; they will reject you; they will think you're awful." But the truth of the matter is, if you confide in a trusted friend, he or she will probably demonstrate more love, more concern, more compassion than you can imagine.

Sexually abused people seem to be holding their breath, afraid that breathing will upset the delicate balance of their lives. But talking to a trusted Christian friend and letting the secret out is like taking a deep breath of fresh air after not breathing for a long time.

The third step is to attend some sessions with a reputable counselor. Most of us reject this advice because we don't want anyone poking around in our past. But anyone with a past as complicated as that of a sexually abused person needs a trained professional to help sort it out. You need some answers and insights. Counselors are trained to provide a badly needed perspective on such things as why it happened and what caused the unhealthy desires in the offender. A counselor will help you work through your rage, mistrust, and low self-esteem when they flare up. And he or she will teach you how to build bridges of communication to the offender.

Those who have never been sexually abused may find all this difficult to understand or accept. But when you encounter someone with symptoms similar to those mentioned as the seven ramifications of sexual abuse, stop for a moment and ask yourself if this woman might be a victim of abuse. Be patient. Be tender. Don't try to force the secret out of her, but allow opportunities for discussion. Talk a little about unconditional love and try with all your heart to put it into practice.

I take no delight in opening up wounds from the past. And I will not even pretend to understand the depth of pain victims suffer. But God does. And He cares, and many other people can understand because they have felt it too. God has ways of making His love, concern, and compassion real to hurting people. I've been praying that victims will find someone they trust, someone who will help them bear their pain. And I've been praying that those who have been spared sexual abuse will find it in their hearts to be compassionate, to reach out with love and acceptance to people with symptoms of abuse. This world is filled with people in pain. As Christians, we are called to break down barriers and reach out with the healing love of Christ.

TEN
What Causes Homosexuality?

While in southern Indiana to speak at a university, I took some time out to study. I took a bunch of books and papers with me to a little country restaurant, sort of a truck stop, and spread them out on the table. As I was preparing to eat lunch, a bubblegum-chewing waitress bounced up and said, "Whatcha studyin'?"

"Homosexuality," I said. "Do you know anything about it?"

"Oh, my gosh," she said, and there was an immediate barrier between us.

I simply told her I was studying it. I didn't say I was involved in it. I didn't tell her I was interested in her son. I was just studying the subject, but that was enough. Just saying the word *homosexuality*—it makes people nervous.

There is great fear partly because there is great ignorance and disagreement on the subject. Most people are even unsure how to define it. The *American Heritage Dictionary* has a twofold definition: (1) Sexual desire for others of one's own sex. (2) Sexual activity with another of the same sex. (Obviously, males and females can be homosexual, but for the purpose of focus we will concentrate our attention on male homosexuals in the next two chapters.) Embedded in the difference between these two definitions is much controversy: Are people born homo- sexuals or do they choose to become homosexuals? And what makes one a homosexual: A desire or an act? There is a good deal of uncertainty and, consequently, much fear of the subject.

The fear of the subject of homosexuality, or the fear of homosexuals, is called *homophobia*. People with homo- phobia are likely to say such things as, "Look, I don't know anything about homosexuals, and I don't want to learn anything about homosexuals. I don't know any, and if I did, I wouldn't associate with them, so can we change the subject, please?"

I suffered from homophobia for many years of my life. I liked telling stories about gays. I knew some very funny queer jokes, and every time I told one I thought it af- firmed my own masculinity. It removed any doubt about where I stood on the subject. Back in college, if we didn't have anything to do on the weekend, we'd say we were "going into town to beat up some queer." Of course we didn't do it, but the fact that we said it revealed our attitude. I had a serious case of homophobia. I know some Christians who still do.

But then God began to lead certain people into my life that I got to be quite close to. Several times in the context of a trusted relationship, I learned that a Christian broth- er was struggling with homosexuality. In many cases I was the first and sometimes the only person he had ever admitted it to.

Those conversations always started rather oddly.

"Bill, you teach that I really matter to God," a friend would begin. "Do I? Really?"

"Well, sure you do," I would answer, wondering what prompted such a question and what was to follow.

"Do I matter to you? Are we friends?"

"Yes, you matter to me," I would say again.

"Are you just saying that, or do you really mean it?"

"I mean it. OK. What's up? Have you done something really wrong? Have you left your wife? Are you an alcoholic? A drug addict? Did you rob a bank? Embezzle from your employer? What is it? You must think I'm going to reject you for whatever it is you're going to confess to me. Go ahead. Try me."

"Well, Bill, I think I might be a homosexual."

I had prepared myself for anything but that. Those were moments of truth for me. Did this man still matter to God? Did he still matter to me?

To answer those questions for myself, I had to do some serious studying, some serious soul-searching. It didn't take me long to learn just how little I knew about homosexuality. And I suspect that the majority of Christians are right where I was not long ago.

One of the first things I learned is that there is a lot of ignorance and misunderstanding surrounding homosexuality. Before we can cure our homophobia and offer help to homosexuals, we need to clear up our own confusion.

The questions that people ask me most frequently are: (1) What causes homosexuality? (2) Is there any hope for homosexuals? (3) What should my attitude be toward them?

What Causes Homosexuality?

I'm happy to say that I can give the definitive answer to the question, "What causes homosexuality?" The definitive answer is, nobody knows for sure. There are, however, four leading theories.

Theory One: God Made Me This Way

The idea that homosexuals are born, not made, is a widely held belief. Just as some people are born left-handed or brown-eyed, this theory says that certain people are born homosexual, that certain genetic arrangements produce homosexual men and women. This theory is often spread by gay liberationists because it absolves them of all responsibility. They say, "We were born this way" or "God made us this way. It's in our genetic makeup. It's not our fault. We can't change, so everybody must accept homosexuality as an alternate lifestyle."

The scientific evidence that homosexuals have a biological predisposition for homosexuality at birth is scant. Not nonexistent, but scant. One author said, "Attempts to fix the causal factors in the biological have not succeeded. In spite of reports to the contrary, there is no scientific evidence that genetic or endocrine factors are causative in homosexual behavior."

While studying this subject, I read twelve major works on homosexuality and countless periodicals, and I have not found one conclusive, documented study that proves the "born-this-way" hypothesis or the genetic hypothesis. Instead, I found the opposite. In studies of the causes of homosexuality, evidence is rapidly piling up that homosexuality is not a genetic issue. It is not biological or hereditary.

Theory Two: My Mother Made Me Do It

The second theory says that destructive family dynamics early in a child's life lead to homosexual behavior. An example of this is the domineering mother/weak father scenario in which the mother is captain of the ship and the father rides in a little dinghy being towed in its wake. Mother runs the ship and intimidates the crew while father snoozes in his dinghy. When a son is born into a family like that, he has few chances to learn any masculine characteristics from his father. Instead, he learns to acquiesce to the desires and demands of his domineering mother. This undermines his masculinity, erodes his self-confidence, and he soon finds it difficult to relate to male peers. He has none of their skills and none of their savvy. Female peers frighten him, as his mother has, so he withdraws into a shell and fantasizes about real men. He often develops a sexual attraction to what it would be like to be a real man. Therefore, when he sees masculinity he is attracted to it.

This kind of background does not make him a homosexual, but it does make him vulnerable and could lead to a homosexual orientation. He will be confused about his sexuality and how to express it, so he is a prime candidate for a homosexual experiment, which can lead to serious trouble. Study after study reveals that vast numbers of homosexuals had poor relationships with their fathers. The weight of research on homosexuality now favors this theory.

One author listed some destructive early family dynamics that might contribute to homosexuality: (1) homes with an absent father and a smothering mother; (2) homes with a punitive, harsh, cruel father and an overprotective, doting mother; (3) homes with a passive, laid-back father and an overpowering, strong-willed mother; (4) homes with a vulgar father and a prudish mother. And there are several other combinations that could result in sexual and psychological confusion in regard to sexuality.

Notice in these combinations that the destructive dynamic involves both parents. One expert says, "It is practically impossible for homosexuality to result in a home where the child has at least one sound relationship with either parent."

I found that statement fascinating. It agrees with many other experts who believe the same thing. I talk with many timid and fearful single parents who are afraid that because they are raising their children alone the children will become homosexual. These parents seem to have a kind of homophobia about this.

I am not trying to affix blame or to tell parents they did a rotten job if their child's homosexuality resulted from destructive early family dynamics. Most people in marriages that produce homosexual children were doing the best they could for their children. But some destruction happened, though it was unintentional.

As mentioned above, destructive early family dynamics lead to "homosexuality vulnerability," but this vulnerability does not necessarily lead to homosexuality. What frequently tips the scale toward homosexuality is an early seduction experience with a member of the same sex.

Theory Three: Seduction of Innocence
The third theory says homosexuality is caused by an early erotic experience with a person of the same sex. After studying this over the years, I think this is the leading cause of homosexuality. Almost every homosexual I know can readily recall and retell in detail the first homosexual episode with an uncle, an older cousin, a friend down the street.

One homosexual told me his experience. "When I was seven years old my mother began to live in common law with a man who was secretly bisexual. We became really good friends, and one day he took me fishing. Before the day was over I had my first homosexual experience. I remember well the feeling of nausea I had afterward, but my stepfather was an expert, and soon I was able to overcome my feelings of revulsion. I became his secret lover, and by the time I was eight years old I knew and practiced sex acts that would probably turn your stomach."

In our early years we have much confusion about human sexuality. We have great interest and easy arousal, but not much focus to our sexuality. This theory says that when a young person has a series of erotic sexual experiences with someone of the same gender it tends to direct his sexuality down a homosexual path.

So in a way, heterosexuals become homosexuals through experimentation, through exciting experiences with older homosexuals. Once the direction is set and the behavior is reinforced, the pattern becomes increasingly difficult to break.

One of my homosexual friends explained to me his early family dynamics. It illustrates how destructive family dynamics and an early erotic experience worked together to create homosexual desires in him.

He grew up in a family with a harsh father who was rarely home. When he was home, he was distant and cruel. His mother, who was doting, overpowering, and smothering, taught him to clean, cook, knit, and crochet. He now realizes the damage that did. By the time he entered elementary school he had no athletic ability whatsoever; he was intimidated by men and other boys because he had rarely been around any; and he didn't understand even the rudiments of masculinity. His classmates viewed him as effeminate and sissified, and he became reclusive and increasingly introverted. Many years later, an attractive, friendly boy down the street took an interest in him. After being approved and fondled by this older boy, and after enjoying a few highly erotic sexual experiences with him, sexual confusion set in and then gave way to homosexual drives that plagued this fellow for the next twenty years.

In my research and in my friendships with homosexuals inside and outside the church, I have seen that pattern over and over again. Destructive early family dynamics followed by an early seduction experience by a relative or a neighbor tips the sexuality scale toward homosexuality.

I read a fascinating study of a poll taken by an expert trying to determine how many active homosexuals considered themselves to have been born that way. Eighty-five percent of those surveyed said they felt their homosexuality was a learned behavior because of destructive early dynamics and an early seduction by another person.

When I meet a homosexual now my first question is usually, "Who started you?" And they can answer me. Then I ask them, "What would have happened to you and to your sexuality had your path not crossed your uncle's? Or your cousin's? Or your stepfather's? What might have happened to you?" And the bells start going off. They say, "Maybe, maybe, maybe."

Theory Four: It's a Mystery

Some believe that the cause of homosexuality remains a mystery that no one can explain. One man wrote, "Even though I was raised in the church, had gone to Christian school, sang in the choir, was president of the young people's society, taught church school, and was striving to become a minister and appeared outwardly to be a model Christian, something was wrong. I was a homosexual. I don't know what caused it, but I am one."

Homosexuality may be caused by a combination of circumstances: a predisposition because of temperament, a family problem, or an early experience. But whatever causes it, we need to try to understand the complexity of it.

Is There Any Hope for Homosexuals?

When I talk with homosexuals I usually give them the bad news/good news verses. First Corinthians 6:9-10 is the bad news. It says, "Do not be deceived; neither fornicators, nor idolators, nor adulterers, nor effeminate, nor homosexuals . . . shall inherit the kingdom of God."

But the good news is found in the very next verse: "And such were some of you; but you were washed, but you were sanctified, but you were justified in the name of the Lord Jesus Christ, and in the Spirit of God."

I do my best to make it clear that homosexual behavior and the homosexual lifestyle are sin, but that God can deliver anyone from any sin.

Let me make one other brief note at this point. The Bible clearly forbids homosexual acts, but it does not ever say that a homosexual temptation, thought, or even a homosexual orientation is sin.

For example, my sexual desire should be focused on my wife. But I have to admit that I'm tempted and I entertain thoughts from time to time about what a sexual experience with another woman would be like. I wrestle with the thought and eventually reject it, saying, "I'm not going to pursue this course of action. I'm not going to think about it anymore. By God's grace I'm going to put that thought aside and return to my wife in my mind."

All of us have those types of thoughts. A person who struggles with homosexual desires may live his entire lifetime with confusion, temptation, and with erotic thoughts about other men, but he can be a Christian. He can even be a minister. He can be a leader in the family of God if he learns, by God's power, how to handle and ultimately reject those thoughts.

Those who struggle with homosexual desires can be delivered from the practice of homosexuality and, I believe, even from most of the thoughts associated with it. But it requires three things.

First, it requires incredible resolve. Leaving the homosexual lifestyle is an unbelievably difficult thing to do. First of all, sex is not the only thing the homosexual is interested in. Like all of us, he is driven by a need for love and acceptance. Because many homosexuals have been labeled from early in their childhood as "different," they have often been rejected by society as well as the church. They retreat into the homosexual community where they oftentimes find a genuine sense of love and caring. This is very difficult to leave.

Second, it requires an uncompromising devotion to Jesus Christ. Because of the need to desire and pursue purity, struggling homosexuals need encouragement and forgiveness when they fall. And this only comes in a saving relationship with Jesus Christ. Victory requires a life filled with His love, His power, His presence.

Third, it requires intense counseling from a Christian counselor. One of my friends has been in counseling for three years, and finally he's leaving his homosexual life-style. But it has taken him three years of intensive counseling to get that far. And he'll probably need support from the body of Christ for the rest of his life.

What Should Our Attitude Be toward Homosexuals?

I spoke this week to a homosexual who had almost lost hope. We were on the phone for nearly an hour. At one point I was almost yelling into the phone because I wanted to communicate with the man so badly.

"There is hope," I screamed. "Don't tell me there isn't. It will be difficult. You'll have to devote yourself to Jesus Christ. And you must find Christian brothers and sisters that you can confide in and pray with—"

"Hybels," he interrupted, "get your head out of the clouds. Christians don't give us gays the time of day. They look down their holy noses, condemn us to hell, secretly hoping that AIDS will kill us all. They're all like that. Why do you think we all end up in the gay community? You chase us out of the church. The only place we find understanding, the only place we find love, is in the gay community."

This time I interrupted him. "I can't speak for every Christian in the world," I said. "I can't even speak for my church. But I can speak for myself, and I'm telling you

that I care. You can confide in me. God has put a love
inside me for struggling brothers and sisters, and I'm not
that fussy about what it is they're struggling with. If it's
materialism, I'll help. Hedonism, I'll help. Marital affairs,
I'll help. I'm not that fussy."

As I see it, there are several positive approaches we
can take toward homosexuals.

First, be their friend. Jesus was called a friend of sinners. I'd love to have that put on my tombstone. "Bill
Hybels, friend of sinners." To me that captures the heart
of a true believer. Our compassion should not be a form
of condescending love, but a standing alongside the homosexual as a fellow sinner. As Paul stated, "If not for
the grace of God, I would be in the same place." It must
be love with humility.

The homosexual is looking, perhaps more than anything else, for an unconditional acceptance: "Can you
love me as I am?" Most homosexuals have been rejected
all their lives and have sought refuge in the homosexual
community for a sense of caring. As Christians, we are
called to unconditionally love. We must demonstrate a
hatred of sin, but a deep love for the sinner. Christ had a
special burden for those who were rejected by society
and living their lives in deep pain. We must follow His
example.

Second, be informed. There is nothing worse than an
ignorant Christian. When we combine ignorance with
passion and conviction we get persecution and intoler-
ance. We'd all be better off if we combined knowledge
with compassion instead. Strip yourself from homophobia. Make an effort to become informed by reading
books and articles on the subject, as well as talking with
those who are trapped in the homosexual lifestyle.
Avoiding the problem does not make the issue disap-
pear, but rather complicates it.

Third, be understanding. Don't jump to any conclusions. Realize the complexity of this issue. I wonder what would have happened to me if a trusted, loving uncle, someone I really believed in, had led me into homosexual activity. Step back and ask yourself that question. Or think about being raised in a home with a domineering mother and a weak or absent father. Are you really sure you would have become heterosexual?

And finally, inspire hope. Homosexuals are dying without hope, and Christians are the only ones who can offer them anything else. We are called to love with a special love those who are dispossessed, powerless, and without hope. Surely, this includes the homosexual. Why then has the Christian community for so long been so silent, so uncaring, so scornful?

ELEVEN
What Cures Homosexuality?

Bruce was at least five years older than me, but he seemed to go out of his way to be my friend. Initially I was flattered that someone older than me, even older than my older brother, would pay attention to me. But before long I began to realize that Bruce was a little bit strange.

We had a pool in our backyard, and during the summer the neighborhood kids spent the majority of their time in it. I began to notice that Bruce had trouble making up his mind about swimming. The first gang of guys would come over and we'd all change into our suits in the bathhouse and then head for the pool. A while later a few more guys would come and Bruce would get out of the pool and get dressed while they were undressing. He would go home for a while and then come back and undress again when more guys came. He would swim a few laps and then head for the bathhouse again. I remember thinking that Bruce spent more time in the bathhouse than he did in the pool.

Then Bruce began inviting me to magic shows that he would put on in his basement. He always promised that a whole gang of guys was coming, but I was always the only one there. And usually his parents weren't home.

Sometimes when I was outdoors, Bruce would call me over to his bedroom window. We would talk through the screen for a while and then I'd get bored and leave, which always seemed to make him sad. I couldn't put my finger on it, but there was something unusual about Bruce.

One night at the supper table my dad announced that he wanted to have a meeting with my brother and me. We went to our room and waited impatiently to find out who had done what wrong.

"What'd you do?" I asked my brother, trying to get an idea of what was coming.

When my father finally entered our room, he sat on my desk. With uncharacteristic nervousness he began to tell us that God made boys to be attracted to girls and He made girls to be attracted to boys. I almost burst out laughing. I thought he was kidding. I couldn't believe we were going to get birds and bees talk from my father. He didn't know it, but I was already quite experienced with the neighborhood girls. I was only in fifth grade, but I knew the difference between boys and girls.

But he continued with something neither my brother nor I expected.

"But some boys are queer," he said. "Some boys are strange. Some boys are weird. Do you follow me?"

Our mouths dropped open. That was new information for both of us.

"Queers try to undress other boys. Queers try to talk them into doing weird things with their bodies." And then he said, "I've got a hunch that Bruce next door is a queer. And if he or any other guy ever tries anything with you two, punch his lights out. Don't let it happen. Follow me?" And with that he left the room, ending our crash course on homosexuality.

For a long time I thought I had learned everything I needed to know about homosexuality in that little session. Some people are strange; stay away from them. If they make advances, deck 'em. And so I proceeded down life's path, doing what most straight people do in regard to homosexuals: I ridiculed them every chance I got.

But then a close friend tried to commit suicide, and I found out he was a homosexual. For the first time I had to deal with the fact that someone I really loved, someone I really cared for, was gay.

And so God dealt with me about my attitude toward homosexuals. I knew I was going to have to change my heart and mind on the subject because my friend needed my help. Homosexuality was no longer a joking matter.

After I announced I was going to preach on homosexuality, several people from my church took me aside and said, sometimes with tears in their eyes, "You know, I'm really looking forward to your sermon on homosexuality." Then they would walk away, leaving behind the echo of their weak cry for help.

I have seen God do some miraculous work in this area in people's lives. One man wrote to me: "Three years ago when you gave your message on homosexuality, I came and I was all ears. It gave me the courage to finally come out of the shadows and tell somebody about my problems in this area." He then described how he found help, and ended his letter by saying, "Now, three years later, I find myself healthier and happier than I ever thought I could be. And God has been so faithful. And last I feel a measure of freedom from the bondage that had such a hold on me. Tell the homosexuals that there is hope. Remind them that they matter to God."

So I am writing to say that there is hope. We all matter to God, regardless of our sexual preferences. I am writing to say that we all need to deal with our collective case of homophobia. Homophobia is best cured by communicating accurate information about homosexuality to dispel the myths. Two of those myths I wish to address are: homosexuals live happy lives, and homosexuals cannot change.

Myth One: Homosexuals Lead Happy Lives

Conservative estimates say that there are fifteen million homosexuals in the United States. We call it "the gay community," but it is anything but gay. The suicide rate among homosexuals is estimated to be ten times higher than among heterosexuals. One author suggests that one half of all suicides in the United States are committed by homosexuals.

The latest Kinsey report claims that one in five homosexuals has attempted suicide. That's how I found out that one of my friends is homosexual. I got a call in the middle of the night that he had taken too many pills. I raced over to his apartment and started dragging him out to my car to take him to the emergency room.

"Just forget it," he said. "I'm gay. Let me die."

One of the reasons many homosexuals are so desperate and despondent is fear—a kind of fear that straight people have a difficult time relating to.

First, they fear being found out by parents, spouses, friends, employers, or church leaders. That fear has an almost paralyzing effect on homosexuals. They live with a gnawing horror that doesn't go away. They fear being ostracized, rejected, ridiculed, and hated by their whole world and especially by the people they love.

Second, they live with the fear of disease. One of my homosexual friends told me about his recent scare. "Bill, last week I discovered red spots all over my genitals. I had to wait a week before I could see a doctor. Thank God, it was only a rash. But, Bill, knowing me, some day I'll get AIDS and die."

Sexually transmitted diseases are rampant among homosexuals. One estimate said that 75 percent of the homosexual community has had or carries some form of venereal disease. Many are well acquainted with hepatitis in both its A and B forms. Though serious and sometimes life-threatening, hepatitis is not the major problem of homosexuals today. The AIDS epidemic tops the list of homosexual concerns. Some of the studies I read about the spread of AIDS were like science fiction horror stories.

Just a few years ago there were only a few hundred confirmed cases; now there are hundreds of thousands, and some reports say that millions are carrying the virus and don't even know it. The number of people being infected by AIDS is doubling every six months.

One of the reasons the homosexual population is so prone to such massive multiplications of sexually transmitted diseases is because of the promiscuity that often goes with the homosexual lifestyle.

Over the course of a lifetime, the average homosexual male will have between five hundred and one thousand sexual encounters with different men. It's less for lesbians. They have fewer casual episodes or sexual encounters. These sexual episodes usually include three sexual activities: sodomy (anal sex), fellatio (oral sex), and oral/anal contact.

These activities, combined with a vast number of sexual partners, make homosexuals highly vulnerable to disease. One doctor said that an active homosexual is 365 times more likely to catch a sexually transmitted disease than a heterosexual. That is why AIDS is spreading so rapidly through the homosexual community. And because bisexuals are transmitting the disease into the heterosexual community, there is no telling where the epidemic will end.

One report I read said that if something miraculous doesn't happen to stop this disease there won't be any homosexuals, bisexuals, prostitutes, or intravenous drug users ten years from now.

Personally, I don't view AIDS as God's specialized plague on homosexuals any more than I view lung cancer as God's plague on cigarette smokers. I see it more as a "reap what you sow" principle in action. Besides, many nonhomosexuals contract AIDS and it's seldom found in the lesbian community. If God were to send a plague to judge homosexuality, I think it would be more focused than it is.

Third, homosexuals live in fear of violence. They are afraid that other homosexuals will turn on them, beat them, and sexually abuse them. I'll never forget the call I received from one of my homosexual friends.

I recognized his voice right away. And I recognized the urgency in it. "What's the matter?" I asked.

He then recounted the story of how he had had his arm broken by another homosexual who was into violent forms of sexual sado-masochism. "This kind of thing happens a lot," he explained when I expressed my shock. "You never know when someone you're having a sexual encounter with is going to turn on you."

Sometime after that I received a call from another homosexual friend. He cried as he recounted the story of how he had been severely beaten in a parking garage in downtown Chicago during a homosexual experience.

"I'm going back there tonight," he said "and I'm scared."

"Then don't go back," I said, stating what I thought was an obvious and logical response.

"But I want to," he said.

That conversation confirmed what I had read in books and magazines and had observed in other homosexuals: The intensity of the homosexual desire is unbelievable. Heterosexuals have strong desires, but from what I can gather, they're not as intense as homosexual lust.

Fourth, homosexuals live with the fear of aging. As one despairing homosexual put it, "Who wants an old faggot?" The market value goes down. The older, less attractive homosexuals are discarded like used tissue paper. In many cases, the homosexual lifestyle is degenerative. A recent poll showed that 37 percent of homosexuals are involved in sado-masochism; 22 percent in humiliation; 22 percent in anal insertion of large objects, such as arms, bottles, and nightsticks; 23 percent said they played with bodily wastes; and 83 percent said they had oral/anal contact. The further one goes into the homosexual lifestyle, the more bizarre, dangerous, and sickening it gets.

Many aging homosexuals can only look forward to subjection to deviant forms of sexual activity. They have no spouse to come home to. No kids around the footstool. No white picket fences. There are few happily-ever-afters for the aging homosexual. It's a dark road that gets darker as the years go by.

Fifth, homosexuals live with the fear of God. True, some homosexuals have been so thoroughly deceived in these matters that they have seared consciences. They have no conscious awareness that they will someday have to give an account of their lives to the holy God. But the vast majority of people in the homosexual community, male and female, have heard sometime, somewhere, that God forbids homosexual activities.

In seven different places in the Old and New Testaments God clearly forbids homosexual acts. To make the Bible say something different, we would have to rip those pages out of it. It's there in black and white. And many homosexuals know that. And the guilt some of them feel is unbelievable.

One of my friends called me recently and asked what hell was like.

"Are you doing a Bible study?" I asked.

"No, I'm planning on going there. Tell me what it's like because I'm going there. I know I am."

He was familiar with the passages on homosexuality: Romans 1; 1 Corinthians 6:9; Leviticus 18. He knows that God is holy and will not tolerate sin. So he lives with a sword poised over his head, never knowing when it will fall and he will be found out, contract a deadly disease, become a victim of violence, grow old and unattractive, or face God's wrath.

And beyond all this they have the fear that they will never be able to change. The level of hopelessness in homosexuals is unbelievable. They are some of the most despairing people on earth.

Myth Two: Homosexuals Cannot Change

The myth that homosexuals cannot change gets a lot of media attention. And many homosexuals believe it. From the time of their earliest memories they have thought of themselves as different from other people. Many don't know why, but they surmise that they were born that way. Many don't know about destructive early family dynamics. Many think their family life was normal. It was all they knew. But members of the same sex ostracize them, reject them, and ridicule them, and members of the opposite sex intimidate them. Along the way many were seduced by someone of the same sex and had a highly erotic experience. Eventually it became a pattern of life. This led to an incredible amount of fear, a boatload of guilt, and a bleak future.

Is it any wonder that so many homosexuals are despondent, paranoid, and overcome by feelings of hopelessness? I have developed an enormous amount of compassion for homosexuals. In many cases I think I'm the only straight friend some of them have. I never condone their homosexual behavior, but I empathize with their agony. And I offer them hope, God's hope.

The Bible says there is hope for the homosexual. First Corinthians 6 lists the sinners who will not inherit the kingdom of God, and it includes homosexuals. But it also includes words of hope: "And such were some of you; but you were washed, but you were sanctified, but you were justified in the name of the Lord Jesus Christ, and in the Spirit of our God" (v. 11).

Some were delivered. Some found the way out. Some stopped their homosexual sin. The Bible says specifically than there is a way out for homosexuals—at least a way out of the homosexual behavior. Scripture also gives us more general promises of hope: "Greater is He who is in you than he who is in the world" (1 John 4:4); "I can do all things through Him who strengthens me" (Phil. 4:13).

Jesus taught that things which are impossible for us are possible through Him. There is hope for the homosexual. But along with hope comes reality: the sobering reality than the way to recovery is a long, difficult, and painful road.

The homosexuals I know who are being successful in their attempts at sexual reorientation, or at least sexual control, have three things in common. First, they have a strong, unswerving commitment to Jesus Christ. One secular expert in the field of homosexuality wrote in his study that he rarely sees progress in the life of a homosexual struggling toward wholeness without God. The homosexuals I know who are finding their way to sexual health have committed themselves to Christ in such a doggedly persevering way that their determination and devoutness inspires and challenges me.

Second, they establish a long-term relationship with a professional therapist. I have never met a homosexual or a lesbian who became sexually reoriented, or sexually whole, without the careful, long-term assistance of a knowledgeable therapist. I'm not saying that God can't do miracles, but it seems to me that He most often uses knowledgeable therapists as His agents of assistance. Early family dynamics must be understood and worked out, learned patterns have to be unlearned, and the anger, self-hate, and rejection have to be resolved. There's a ton of work awaiting the homosexual who wants out. But it is a good kind of work. It's the kind that makes building blocks with which to build a whole new future.

Third, they find an accepting environment where they can make progress. A dream of mine has been to have the kind of church that offers a supportive, understanding environment where personal battles for wholeness of any kind can be waged. Generally speaking, I'm pleased with the kind of warmth, tolerance, and openness that people in our church have for one another. But I am praying that we get over our homophobia. I don't like hearing gay jokes. Sometimes I wonder if Christians just put up a stage prop along the road that looks like a refuge for sinners. We use it to trick them into coming through the door, but once they're inside they find nothing but accusers who call themselves saints.

We are all battling something: greed; envy; lust; pride; or addictions to drugs, alcohol, pornography, or homosexuality. So why don't we all just roll up our sleeves and offer one another whatever assistance and encouragement we can. Christians need to be God's understanding, usable, and humble agents of healing in the lives of struggling brothers and sisters. We need to realize that it is better to be a homosexual aware of sin and struggling to overcome it than to be proud that we don't have a problem with it.

There is hope for the homosexual. There is hope in Christ, hope through the help of a competent therapist, and hope in an accepting, caring community. But every homosexual must choose that hope. They can stay on the road leading to fear, guilt, sickness, and despair, or they can take the crossroad back to wholeness.

They can step out of the shadows into the light. There is hope, but they must make the first move.

That is a difficult step, not just for homosexuals but all those who have committed some form of sexual sin. Whether it takes the form of homosexuality, incest, adultery, or fornication, sexual sin clings to the heart. Perhaps more than any other form of sin, it blocks out the potential for the light of God's forgiveness. Until that light can be clearly seen, the darkness is deep indeed.

TWELVE
Forgiveness and Overcoming

At 2:30 in the morning, the woman came to meet with the elders of our church. She was exhausted, offtrack spiritually, out of tune in her marriage, and contemplating adultery. She knew she needed help.

The elders assembled, and we pleaded with her to reconsider. After pressing for reasons about why she was contemplating being unfaithful to her husband, she finally said: "God will forgive me if I repent later." Incensed, one of the elders rose from his chair and said, "Do you think God is a fool? Who do you think He is that you can blatantly disobey and then casually repent and claim His forgiveness?"

I will carry the memory of that evening with me until the day I die. It was one of the most dramatic moments I've experienced because I came to a sudden realization: I thought the same way as that woman thought. One of the most clever ploys of the evil one is to get us to think we can be unfaithful to our holy God. All we have to do is repent later. God has to forgive us because He says He will. We've got God on the hook. That evening was a turning point in my own mind.

That woman, and I would guess most of us, has an inaccurate view of the effects of sin. First of all, sin has natural consequences. God has implemented a structure to the universe and a natural order, and He has given us His rules to outline that design. Anything that steps outside of that order is sin. And it costs. For example, God has told us that He designed sex to be enjoyed inside the bond of marriage. When we violate that design, we suffer consequences: disease, guilt, ruined relationships, and the list goes on and on. When we sin as believers, we risk God's love—His deep desire that we should have the best and His passionate, jealous concern for our well-being. He will stop at nothing, including harsh discipline, to bring us back to our senses. Christians risk much when they sin.

But that's not the worst of it. In God's eyes, we are committing cosmic treason every time we sin. He has made it clear in His Word that sin is a violation of His very being and will not be tolerated. God always associates sin with death. When Adam sinned in the garden, he was given the sentence of death. Romans 6:23 states: "For the wages of sin is death." In James 1:15 we read, "And sin, when it is full-grown, gives birth to death."

I love the parable that Jesus tells in Matthew 18 because it so accurately portrays the cost of sin. Let me review the story and paraphrase. An extremely wealthy businessman declared to some of his vice presidents, accountants, and consultants that he suspected trouble. He thought that someone might have a hand or two in the till. So he ordered an audit and now he wants to announce the results. His fears were well-founded. One of his key men has embezzled an astronomical amount of the boss' money—maybe $10 million.

Jesus makes it clear that this man didn't simply make an accounting error. Instead, it was used for heavy-duty sin—a wine, women, song, and live-it-to-the-hilt type of embezzlement. He had squandered all of the money, and he had nothing left. He did not put money away in a Swiss bank account and now, the day of judgment at hand, he has no way to pay back the debt.

The boss, of course, calls in the man to give an account of his actions. He has to go in and admit that out of greed and covetous passion, he blatantly cheated his long-time boss. So he enters, trembling and humiliated. You can hear his stomach growl. He has a headache the size of the Grand Canyon. He is sweating profusely. He fears his boss' condemnation and, following that, a jail sentence.

Their eyes meet as the boss hands down the sentence: "Sell the man and his family into slavery and let him attempt to work off a portion of the debt for a lifetime. And then, let his children pay off a portion of his debt for their lifetimes; and sell their offspring into slavery for as many generations as it takes to pay off the astronomical debt."

The words pierce to the man's soul. He realizes the consequences of his actions. He knows that he is doomed, that he has not a shred of hope. Maybe for the first time in his life, he feels grief over his behavior. Now the embezzler does something that shocks everyone who has gathered in the boardroom: He falls on his face and asks for forgiveness. He doesn't really believe it will work but, at this point, he doesn't have many options. Splattering his face on the floor doesn't seem too bad as a last-ditch effort. So, he cries out for mercy.

There are giggles in the room. Someone mutters underneath his breath: "Dreamer. You will receive your just punishment. Do you expect anyone to have mercy on a person like yourself?" Then comes the real surprise. The hard-nosed, self-made billionaire looks at the man, his eyes filling with tears, and says, "I forgive you. You are free to go."

Who Pays the Debt?

That was certainly a surprising and compassionate act. But consider what happened when the meeting disbanded and everyone went home: the boss was left with a $10 million debt. His forgiveness cost him dearly. He absorbed the debt himself. What a picture of God as forgiver. God could not just wave a magic wand and eliminate the problem of sin. Anyone who thinks that does not clearly understand the depths of the problem of evil. God could forgive us only because He absorbed the astronomical debt Himself.

As we have seen earlier, the Bible is clear that the price of sin is death. So Jesus, after being crucified on a cross, was placed in a tomb. God's very own Son, although sinless, died because our sin demanded it. He was sacrificed to cover our sins. There was no other way to extend forgiveness to us but to absorb the debt. The Bible says that without "the shedding of blood there is no remission for sin" (Lev. 17:11). And so it pleased the Father to allow Christ to bleed and die. That's what it cost Him to cover our moral debt. He loved us that much.

If we realize the depth of God's sacrifice for our sins, we will understand two truths: God loves us very much, and God hates sin very much. And those two principles will change our lives.

That is why that woman's attitude about committing adultery affected me so much. We must never treat sin with such a flippant attitude. How dare we presume on God's forgiveness when we fail to understand the cost of our sinful actions? There is no such thing as easy sin, easy repentance, and easy forgiveness.

That is the one extreme—presuming on the forgiveness of God. The other extreme is equally dangerous—not accepting the forgiveness of God. This reaction seems especially common with sexual sin. The guilt and the damage associated with sexual sin are so intense, and cling so deeply in the heart, that people often feel they have either committed the unpardonable sin or they need to, in some way, do penance to earn their forgiveness.

False Guilt

Guilt, for the most part, is a good thing. It makes us face our sin and understand it for what it is: a heinous crime against God. However, a sense of false guilt can cripple us, even make us self-destructive. It is important to us to realize that we are going to sin. We will never entirely escape the old sin nature until we get to heaven. The Apostle Paul, after doing things he did not want to, cried out in desperation: "Oh, wretched man that I am!" He felt the tremendous weight of guilt. He understood what it meant to sin against a holy God.

But Paul's next thought takes a curious turn: "Therefore, there is now no condemnation for those who are in Christ Jesus" (Rom. 8:1). Not only did Paul clearly understand the depth of his sin, but he also understood the incredible depth of God's forgiveness. He acknowledged the sting of his guilt as well as the healing compassion of God's love. We must do the same.

The evil one would love to use guilt to destroy us. In the Bible, one of the names for Satan is the Accuser. Day and night, he stands before God and accuses the brethren. In other words, he seeks to intensify the guilt to the point of paralysis. He wants us to think that because of our sin we have become useless to God's kingdom. He knows full well a thoroughly discouraged Christian is an utterly useless Christian.

When a believer does something that causes regret, the evil one goes to work immediately. He whispers in our ear: "Wake up, pal, you are now condemned in the sight of God. This sin was the last straw. Do you think God will forgive you of *that*? No amount of pleading will get you forgiven this time. You stepped over the line."

Spiritual Paralysis

In many cases, one of two things happen when we believe Satan's lies: The believer sinks in a pool of despair and self-pity, or he tries to earn God's forgiveness by an extended display of self-crucifixion. Both actions display a deficient understanding of the depth of God's forgiveness.

This kind of unresolved guilt does not go away with time. Not long ago a businessman came into my office and broke down and wept. Thirteen years ago while on a business trip he had committed adultery with a woman he met in a lounge. For all those years, he carried the burden of the guilt. His marriage was shattered and he could barely pray. "In the middle of your sermons," he told me, "sometimes I feel so awful I just want to say, 'God, kill me. Send me to hell. I can't live like this.' "

This is not an isolated example. There are many who suffer from the incredible intensity of the guilt of sexual sin. Just two of the examples I have dealt with give you some kind of idea of the depth of the intensity:

• A young Christian man felt called into Christian work, perhaps as a youth pastor, Sunday School teacher, missionary, or minister, but refused the call because he thought God could never use him after his past sexual sins.

• A young pregnant woman lived month after month in a near panic, fearing her child would be born abnormal as punishment for her sexual sin during her high school prom night.

This is where the evil one wants us—paralyzed by fear. But the Bible says that perfect love casts out fear. That is what forgiveness is: a demonstration of perfect love.

The Depth of God's Love

If we understand properly what the consequences of sin are and what it cost God to accept the debt, we will better understand the height and depth and breadth of His love for us. The motivation for God's forgiveness is love. His means of expressing that love was Christ on the cross, bleeding and dying to cover our sins.

In the awful shadow of the Cross, there shines a bright light. Forgiveness is available. We need to understand the awesome work of God in accomplishing our salvation. It is in the light of the Cross that we must fall to our knees, acknowledge our sin, and accept His great love and forgiveness.

Denial, self-pity, or penance will never relieve our guilt. It is only by God's grace through the work of Christ: "In Him we have redemption through His blood, the forgiveness of sins, in accordance with the riches of God's grace" (Eph. 1:7).

Accepting God's grace is at the heart of what it means to be forgiven. One woman wrote me: "I had been an abused child, an abused wife, almost killed, divorced, an alcoholic, a neglectful mother, financially and morally bankrupt. In my narrow perception, a Christian had to have 2.5 perfect children, a 3-bedroom, 2-bath home, a sane loving partner, a successful career, and attend church every Sunday.

"I have been plagued with that 'Christian picture' perception. Knowing full well I can never atone for past sins, I was certain a full Christian life would never be mine. I could not imagine a God that did not keep a scorecard. Of course, Satan attacked me constantly on this issue."

After a particularly painful day, this woman remembers hearing a message on God's grace. "Exhausted and broken from carrying my burden, I really heard the message. I picked up my Bible and started reading anything and everything on grace. Why had I not seen it before? The tears of despair turned to tears of joy. At last, I understood."

The Grace of God

The woman had lived on a treadmill of guilt. Her inability to accept forgiveness offered through the grace of God created incredible internal turmoil. In order to compensate for the lack of peace, she started a cycle of sin and self-destructive behavior. She tried to drink herself into oblivion. She abused her children. Her inability to accept forgiveness led to a lack of self-esteem, which led her to try to eliminate that void with pleasure seeking and self-destructive behavior. That is not an unusual cycle.

Another woman, who could not find forgiveness for her divorce, found herself heading into more sin. "I don't know who I am anymore, or where I am heading," she wrote to me. "I'm scared. Feeling so down, worthless, alone, etc., I didn't listen to God prompting me . . . and I'm very ashamed to say I committed adultery. I really blew it. I never dreamed I could or would ever do something so awful as that. I feel so unclean, and I should."

When we fail to accept forgiveness, the cycle becomes a vicious one. Lack of self-esteem. Sin. More guilt. Lower self-esteem. More sin. Lower self-esteem. And so on.

The answer? Accept God's great love and forgiveness now. Because of Christ's work on the cross, God's forgiveness is complete. The duration is eternal for those who acknowledge and repent of their sin. Try to read these verses like it was the first time you had ever read them. They will amaze you.

• "Though your sins are like scarlet, they shall be as white as snow" (Isa. 1:18).

• "As far as the east is from the west, so far has He removed our transgressions from us" (Ps. 103:12).

• "For I will forgive their wickedness and will remember their sins no more" (Jer. 31:34).

• "If we confess our sins, He is faithful and just and will forgive us our sins and purify us from all unrighteousness" (1 John 1:9).

There is no need to wallow in self-pity or punish ourselves. Forgiveness, not in part but in whole, is available.
God offers us the chance to start again and get at the
business of loving God and promoting His kingdom.

Remember the businessman that Jesus talked about in
Matthew 18? Think how astonished he must have been to
hear those words: "I forgive you." In Ephesians 1:4 we
read that we will be presented blameless before God. Can
you picture that? You . . . me . . . standing someday
when the moral audit comes down on judgment day.
Jesus stands with His arm around you and He says,
"He's blameless. Covered. I absorbed the consequences
of his sin." And that holds true whether you cheated on
a quiz or on your wife. It all is covered by the Blood.
Amazing, isn't it?

Once we begin to understand the love and forgiveness
of God, all we can do is to scratch our heads with the
Apostle Paul: "But God demonstrates His own love for
us in this: While we were still sinners, Christ died for us.
Since we have now been justified by His blood, how
much more shall we be saved from God's wrath through
Him!" (Rom. 5:8-9)

Dealing with the Real World
Once forgiven, we still have to deal with the real world.
Forgiveness does not mean God places you in Shangri-la.
You still must deal with the consequences of your sin.
Forgiveness doesn't change that. You must understand
that your behavior has created deep hurt and steps must
be taken to resolve that pain. That's the bad news. The
good news is that you can face those consequences with
a regenerated spirit, knowing that God has forgiven you.
That gives a new resolve and sense of courage.

As discussed earlier, sexual sin has consequences that
tend to linger. Because God designed sex to be such a
deep communicator of love and respect, it stands to rea-

son that it also creates deep division and pain when abused. People get hurt, oftentimes critically. One woman, a victim of sexual abuse as a child, signed a letter she wrote to me, "Forever hurting." She believes there is no cure for her pain.

Those who commit adultery find it difficult, sometimes impossible, to repair the damage done to their spouses. Trust has been violated, and it will take no small effort to regain what has been lost.

Seek Forgiveness

Once a sexual sin is committed, seeking God's forgiveness is only the first step, although a critical one. The one who sexually abuses another must seek out the forgiveness of the person abused. In the case of adultery, for example, the guilty party must ask for forgiveness from both the spouse and the new partner. Much is at stake.

Asking for forgiveness from the injured parties acknowledges your sense of wrongdoing and their deep hurt. You are saying to them: "I know what I have done has hurt you. I want to understand your pain and help to resolve it. I am taking responsibility for the consequences of my behavior." Healing cannot take place until you recognize the existence of wounds.

Seeking forgiveness also allows the abused to extend forgiveness, which is often difficult. And often healing. Forgiveness in the biblical sense is a cycle. The one forgiven seeks to forgive. Since we have all been forgiven much by the grace of God, we all have much we can forgive others of.

Asking for and receiving forgiveness is only a start. The process will be long and difficult; don't expect a quick cure. Sexual sin carries a ton of consequences, but God is a God who specializes in reconstruction. The marriage ripped apart by adultery can be put back together again—in some cases, better than before. The man who wrestles with homosexual desires can keep himself from sinful behavior. The child who was sexually abused by her father can openly and honestly declare: "I love you."

I know because I've seen it. From the ashes of broken lives and relationships, God does His most impressive work. When we acknowledge how hopeless the situation is, we can obtain our greatest hope. It's not easy. It takes an incredible amount of courage, discipline, patience, and internal resolve. Long-standing patterns of sin will have to be dealt with. You should seek professional counseling and keep yourself accountable to someone. But if you take it one small step at a time, God can rebuild the foundations of trust, communication, and sensitivity that were destroyed by sexual sin. That's just the kind of God He is. We must begin at the step of forgiveness—accepting God's, asking for it from the injured party, and extending it to the one who has committed the sexual sin.

The Victim

Even now as I write, I can hear words of protest from those whose lives have been devastated by sexual sin: "My husband ran off with another woman and left me with three kids, no job, and a monthly house payment. You expect me to forgive him?" Or: "My wife said that I didn't meet her desires; that I provided no sensitivity. So she got involved in a lesbian relationship. She says she needed the tenderness. Do you expect me to forgive her?" Or, from an actual letter I received: "You see, Bill, our marriage has been destroyed twice now by adultery. My husband has been physically and verbally abusive and involved with pornography. A year ago, about six months after I found out he was having an affair with one of my closest friends, he literally attacked me in the shower; choking me, pounding me with his fist and saying, 'I will kill you. You will die.' "

Many victims of sexual sin have died a thousand deaths. Not physically, but emotionally and spiritually. They have felt the searing pain of being abandoned and forsaken. Many write to me and say that they would like to forgive but can't find it within themselves.

One woman, who attends my church, wrote: "The incest I experienced was at the hands of my father. I had been used in different ways to satisfy my father's sexual needs and just before turning four years old, he raped me late one night. My whole little system shut off. I could not walk, talk, or hear for a matter of months." How can you forgive someone like that? For a long time, she did not. She tried to cover up her childhood, repress the anger and dismiss that point in her life as if it never existed. As an adult, she tried to commit suicide twice. She sought help. "While in therapy I've dealt with a flood of repressed anger and rage. And feelings—so many feelings. I feel dirty, ashamed, less than human, guilty, depressed, responsible. Acceptance of my childhood came slowly. I didn't want to believe it was really that way, as if somehow refusing to look at it could change it all."

Through a long period of grieving and pain, she was able to work through some of the issues. Although she says she still feels the tension in her life, God has allowed her to move on. "(I have found) that God is *always* faithful and loving. And He's shown me time and again in my life that painful experiences, illnesses, etc. can be used to help others to reach beyond their own walls of denial.

"So I'm not a victim, nor just a survivor. I'm a miracle! Proof of God's power, mercy, grace, and love because Christ lives in me and because of Him I can accept, forgive, and go on."

The ability to forgive did not come without a cost. God does not expect or want us to merely mouth words of forgiveness. He does not want us to gloss over or ignore the pain. What He does expect us to do is to deal with the problem. Face it head-on. Though that is an extremely painful process, He wants us to do it for our own benefit. The trauma and hurt for victims of sexual sin does not just vanish into thin air.

An unforgiving spirit can be the sign of deeper trouble, which could manifest itself in self-destructive behavior and spiritual paralysis. Though it will probably be the hardest thing you have ever done in your life, you should take steps to deal with the problem. Begin today.

Acknowledge God's Love
The first and, perhaps, most important thing I would like to say to those who have been victimized is: God loves you. Please, please understand that! Because of the rejection you have felt at the hands of another, you might believe that God too could be unfaithful. Please don't make that mistake. God will never forsake you. Turn to Him and pour out your heart to Him. He longs to enter into your pain, wrap you in His loving arms, and heal your shattered life. In order to deal with the pain, you will need His supernatural strength and love. If you are to make genuine steps toward healing, you will need to trust Him like you have never trusted Him in your life.

Deal with False Guilt
One of the most common reactions of victims is to blame themselves. Another victim of sexual child abuse wrote: "The thing that hurts the most is that I have always felt like a guilty party, that somehow I could have stopped him. As an adult and a Christian I now know this is just false guilt, but I spent a lot of years in a torture chamber." We must be careful here. Not all sexual sin is as one-sided as the sexual abuse of children where there is clearly an abuser and a victim. In some sexual sin, the cause and effect can fade into shades of gray. A healthy

introspection is in order. If there is sin on your part, confess it, make steps to correct the patterns, and accept God's forgiveness. Many times, however, blame is improperly owned by the victim. "If" becomes the big word. "*If* I would have done this . . ." "*If* I had stopped that. . . ."

Blame, in combination with feelings of rejection, often can lead to a poor self-esteem. That means problems. Because you do not feel at peace with yourself, you will seek to escape. That could lead to further sin, which could lead to a destructive downward cycle.

Deal With the Rage

Remember the letter from the woman whose husband had committed adultery? She wrote: "In my narrow perception, a Christian had 2.5 perfect children, a 3-bedroom, 2-bath home, a sane loving partner, a successful career, and attended church every Sunday."

Within Christianity, there are many Norman Rockwell pictures on the walls of people's minds. Christians are supposed to act and behave in certain ways. There is a dangerous tendency to paint images of perfection, which is highly destructive to honest communication and the resolution of problems. The tendency is to dismiss all problems and emotions that don't fit into the picture as somehow wrong. Being wrong, they need to be dismissed or covered up; they don't fit with the pretty Christian pictures. I find this scenario to be especially true with sexual sin.

This is extremely unhealthy. Dismissing the problem—along with the anger and guilt associated with it—leads eventually to self-destructive behavior. If the hurt is deep enough, as it often is in sexual sin, the problem could reappear in the form of alcoholism, drug abuse, or even suicidal thoughts. Refusing to deal with the problem can also lead to trouble in other relationships.

Swallowing anger and hate leads to bitterness in the pit of the stomach. In Hebrews 12:15 we read, "See to it that no one misses the grace of God and that no bitter root grows up to cause trouble and defile many." Along similar lines, "Get rid of all bitterness, rage and anger, brawling and slander, along with every form of malice. Be kind to one another, forgiving each other, just as Christ forgave you" (Eph. 4:31-32). Forgiving each other is the key to resolving bitterness. But, once again, the question surfaces: how do we genuinely forgive after such deep hurt?

Grieve

The reason we run from our problems by dismissing and repressing feelings of anger and hate is because they are painful to deal with. We quite naturally seek to protect ourselves. Yet the Bible's answer to deep hurt is not self-protection but, in a very real sense, self-abandonment. God invites us not to put up walls but, rather, to tear down barriers that keep us from experiencing our pain and disappointments. God is asking us to identify the pain, embrace it, and feel it completely.

He wants us to grieve thoroughly—to feel terrible for however long it takes. Counselors tell me that this grieving process can take as long as three to six months. In many cases, it feels like dying.

There are no acceptable alternatives. It is necessary to free ourselves. One woman, sexually abused by her brother, wrote: "I am 27 years old and have not seen my brother in seven years and know the hatred and bitterness I feel toward him. What I feel toward him is so strong that I don't care if I ever see him again." Can you imagine the intensity of those emotions? Is this not in some ways a slower and more painful experience than dealing with the root of the problem?

The beginning process for forgiveness has little to do with the well-being of the person who hurt you. It has more to do with your mental, physical, and spiritual health. Through your grieving, God wants to protect and cleanse you.

Establish an Open Line of Communication

The hurt you feel must be communicated to the one who hurt you—not to punish that person, but for the purposes of honesty and awareness. We must communicate our pain. It is part of the process of extending forgiveness. In some cases, this is especially difficult. It is at this juncture that God can use professional counselors to help you heal. They are skilled in understanding the ways strong emotions or faulty thought can block wholeness and healing. Even victims of sexual child abuse are often brought to the point of being able to communicate their hurt to the abusive parent.

Maybe you think that you don't need help. You think that you are stronger than some victims or that your circumstances are not as bad as some of those we've talked about. Don't fool yourself. If you are a victim of some type of sexual sin, you have been wounded.

Please don't be afraid to seek help. The stakes are too high to try to go through this thing alone. For many individuals, the road to recovery is negotiated with the wisdom of a skilled, professional counselor. The importance of this step cannot be minimized. An open line of communication is often the channel through which healing occurs.

"I Love You."

God is full of surprises. He delights in accomplishing the impossible. I know that many of you are saying right now, "But, Bill, you don't know how *I* feel. You can't feel *my* pain. You don't know what *my* wife did. You'll never know how bad *I* hurt. If you did, you'd know why *I* can't forgive."

That's true. I don't know your pain. I have, however, seen others demonstrate an incredible amount of courage in very painful circumstances. They have resolved to take steps to embrace their grief and, through the supernatural assistance of God, have finally let it go. The husband of a woman who was abused as a child wrote to me of the painful process both of them went through in dealing with her background. He has seen the pain and, to some extent, the tension continues. But he has also seen a miracle of God. "The most beautiful thing I have seen in my life has been when my wife goes to her father, looks him in the eye, and says, 'I love you.' And she really means it."

There's one other thing. Although I don't know your pain, there is Someone who does. Once again, our model is Jesus Christ. On the road to Calvary, He was spit upon, whipped, mocked, and finally hung on a cross to die with two common thieves. In between His painful gasps for breath, He managed to speak these words: "Father, forgive them."

He is still speaking those same words today.

RECOMMENDED RESOURCES

ABORTION
Books and Resources

1. *Abortion's Second Victim,* Pam Koerbel, Victor Books.

2. *Mom I'm Pregnant,* Bev O'Brian, Tyndale.

3. *One Church's Answer to Abortion,* Bill Hybels, Moody Press.

4. *The Least of These, What Everyone Should Know About Abortion,* Curt Young, Moody Press.

5. *Focus on the Family*
   Box 500
   Pomona, CA 91779
   Miscellaneous tapes and material.

PORNOGRAPHY

1. *"Anatomy of a Lust,"* Leadership, February 1982. A copy of this article can be obtained by writing:
   Leadership Article
   Counseling Center

Willow Creek Community Church
67 E. Algonquin Road
South Barrington, IL 60010

2. *Focus on the Family* material available:
   Final report of the Attorney General's Commission
   on Pornography.
   Fact sheet on pornography which includes individuals in Washington you can write to express
   concerns.
   Various tapes and booklets on pornography.

   Write to:
   Focus on the Family
   Box 500
   Pomona, CA 91799

3. *The Mind Polluters*, Jerry Kirk, Thomas Nelson.

HOMOSEXUALITY
Agencies

1. Spatula Ministries
   P.O. Box 444
   LaHabra, CA 90631
   213-691-7369

2. Outpost
   1821 University Ave. South HS-292
   St. Paul, MN 55104
   612-645-2530
   Free monthly publication available.

3. Homosexuals Anonymous
   P.O. Box 732
   Hillsdale, IL 60162
   312-449-3321

4. Focus on the Family
   Pomona, CA 91799

Various tapes on homosexuality.

Books

1. *Growing Up Straight, What Every Family Should Know About Homosexuality*, George A. Rekers, Moody Press.

2. *Where Does a Mother Go to Resign?* Barbara Johnson, Bethany Publications

3. *The Broken Image*, Leanne Payne, Crossway Books.

4. *The Returns of Love*, Alex Davidson, InterVarsity Press.

CHILD ABUSE
Agencies

National Committee for the Prevention of Child Abuse
332 South Michigan Ave.
Suite 950
Chicago, IL 60604-4357

Crisis and referral

1. Child Help USA 1-800-4-A-CHILD

2. Check yellow pages of phone book under: "Social Services" or "Family Services."